*The 500 Hidden Secrets of*

# COPEN

# INTRODUCTION

This book is created to help readers discover the secret local gems that make Copenhagen one of the world's 'most liveable cities' and one of Europe's most exciting centres for design, innovation, and creativity.

Like the Danish culture itself, the ancient harbour city of Copenhagen is full of charming, subtle idiosyncrasies. The aim of this book is to get you started on discovering the best of the real Copenhagen: both the interesting (and delicious) places you should visit, as well as some insights into the people, events, and ideas that have shaped the Danish capital. That's why this book includes not only lists of the 5 best places to sample New Nordic cuisine and the 5 cosiest cafes for a rainy day, but also introduces readers to the 5 icons of Danish modernist architecture, the 5 cultural quirks to know about the Danes, and the 5 most fascinating relics from Copenhagen's past.

To understand what makes Copenhagen one of the world's most trend-setting urban centres, it is essential to sample a few of the city's 5 essential microbreweries, practice implementing the 5 most important rules for cycling in Copenhagen, and browse the latest styles on display at Copenhagen's 5 best shops for modern streetwear. Whether wandering through The Latin Quarter, rowing a kayak in the canals of Christianshavn, strolling the haunted lanes of Assistens Kirkegård, or dining and dancing in The Meatpacking District, you will soon sense that this is a city where people celebrate the simple pleasures of nature, cuisine, and relationships. In fact, that is the very heart of what it means to be a Copenhagener.

# HOW TO USE
# THIS BOOK?

This guide lists 500 things you need to know about Copenhagen in 100 different categories. Most of these are places to visit, with practical information to help you find your way. Others are bits of information that help you get to know the city and its habitants. The aim of this guide is to inspire not to cover the city from A to Z.

The places listed in the guide are given an address, including the neighbourhood (for example Østerbro or Frederiksberg), and a number. The neighbourhood and number allow you to find the locations on the maps at the beginning of the book: first look for the map of the corresponding neighbourhood, then look for the right number. A word of caution however: these maps are not detailed enough to allow you to find specific locations in the city. You can obtain an excellent map from any tourist office or in most hotels. Or the addresses can be located on a smartphone.

Please also bear in mind that cities change all the time. The chef who hits a high note one day can be uninspiring on the day you happen to visit. The hotel ecstatically reviewed in this book might suddenly go downhill under a new manager. The bar considered one of the 5 best places for live music might be empty on the night you visit. This is obviously a highly personal selection. You might not always agree with it. If you want to leave a comment, recommend a bar or reveal your favourite secret place, you can contact the publisher at *info@lusterweb.com*. Or follow *@500hiddensecrets* on Instagram and leave a comment – you'll also find free tips and the latest news about the series there.

# THE AUTHOR

Austin Sailsbury lives and works in Copenhagen. As a freelance writer and creative consultant, Austin has contributed to many international print and web publications, including *Kinfolk Magazine* (US), *RELEVANT Magazine* (US), *The Murmur* (DK) and *Cold North Magazine* (DK). He is also the author of the book *American Getaway: 100 Years of Saints and Sinners at Camp Wandawega* (US).

Over the past decade, Austin has lived in several corners of Copenhagen, from the leafy, historic village of Lyngby, to the bustling, graffiti-chic Nørrebro neighbourhood, to the 'Danish Riviera' of Copenhagen's coastal suburbs. He recommends that visitors intentionally diversify the time they spend in Copenhagen, making sure to visit a variety of the districts outside the busy, well-travelled city centre.

The author wishes to thank all those who shared their insights and tips about the city of Copenhagen. Thanks to Peter Stanners, Nick Scriven, Ben Catford, Alex Kierrumgaard, Peter Balstrup, Isabella Smith, Steve Momsen, Lill Buhl Bersang, and Dieuwertje Visser of Nordic Noir Tours. Without the help of these local experts, the quality and diversity of the following lists of hidden secrets would have been significantly diminished. Thanks also to the book's photographer Tino van den Berg, who braved many days of blustery Danish weather to capture the quirky, colourful character of 'Wonderful Copenhagen'. Thanks to the publishing team at Luster for their guidance and help along the way. Lastly, Austin would like to thank his wife for her help, encouragement, and patience throughout the research and writing of this book.

# COPENHAGEN

*overview*

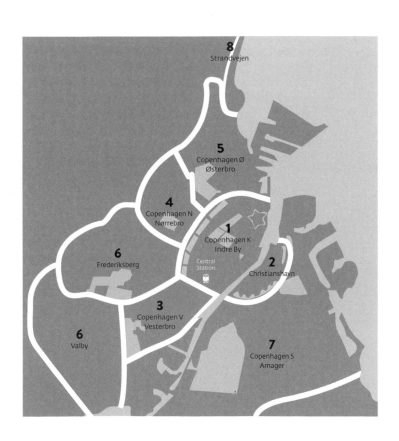

**8**
Strandvejen

**5**
Copenhagen Ø
Østerbro

**4**
Copenhagen N
Nørrebro

**1**
Copenhagen K
Indre By

**6**
Frederiksberg

Central
Station

**2**
Christianshavn

**3**
Copenhagen V
Vesterbro

**6**
Valby

**7**
Copenhagen S
Amager

# Map 1
# COPENHAGEN K
# INDRE BY

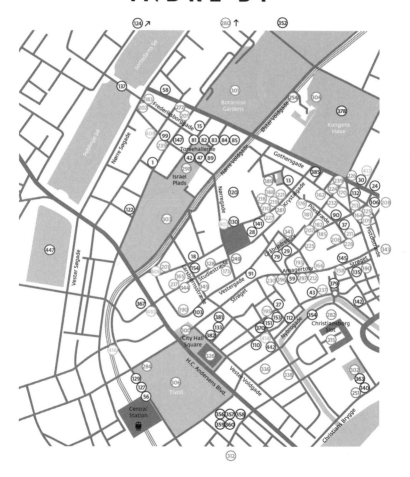

# Map 2
# CHRISTIANSHAVN

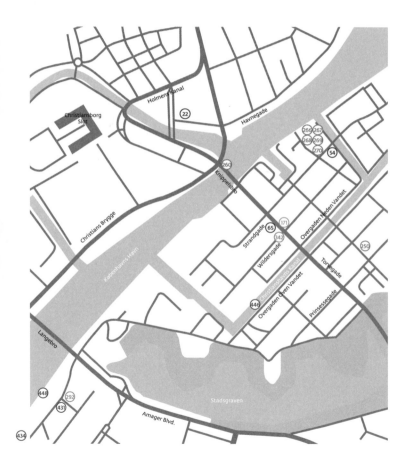

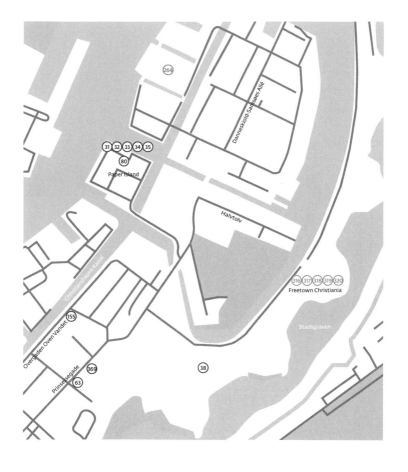

Dannebrog-Samsøes Allé

264

31 32 33 34 35

80

Paper Island

Halvtolv

316 317 318 319 320

Freetown Christiania

Christianshavns Kanal

Stadsgraven

Overgaden Oven Vandet

155

Prinsessegade

369

63

38

# *Map 3*
# COPENHAGEN V
# VESTERBRO

# *Map 4*
# COPENHAGEN N
# NØRREBRO

*Map 5*

# COPENHAGEN Ø
# ØSTERBRO

EAT — **DRINK** — SHOP — BUILDINGS — DISCOVER — **CULTURE** — CHILDREN — SLEEP — **WEEKEND ACTIVITIES** — RANDOM

# Map 6
# FREDERIKSBERG
# & VALBY

# *Map 7*
# COPENHAGEN S
# AMAGER

# Map 8
# STRANDVEJEN

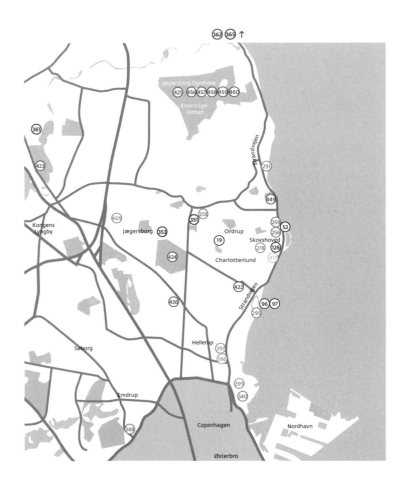

# 100 PLACES TO EAT OR BUY GOOD FOOD

———

# The 5 best places to try
# NEW NORDIC CUISINE

---

### 1 HÖST

**Nørre Farimagsgade 41**
**Copenhagen K** ①
**+45 8993 8409**
*www.cofoco.dk/en/*
*restaurants/hoest*

Winner of 'The World's Best Design Restaurant' in 2013, Höst is Copenhagen's most accessible New Nordic dining experience. With it's ever-evolving seasonal menu, Höst offers up course after course of locally sourced, quirky, and delicious food you won't find anywhere else. Tip: book ahead online.

### 2 RESTAURANT RADIO

**Julius Thomsens Gade 12**
**Copenhagen V** ③
**+45 2510 2733**
*restaurantradio.dk*

Opened by Noma co-founder Claus Meyer, Radio serves exquisite five-course dinners for around 400 kroner. The focus is on sustainably grown, organic vegetables sourced from their own farms.

### 3 AMASS RESTAURANT

**Refshalevej 153**
**Copenhagen K** ①
**+45 4358 4330**
*www.amassrestaurant.com*

Another spinoff from a Noma veteran, the extraordinary Amass Restaurant is led by American chef and owner Matt Orlando. Best reached by a city water bus, Amass is located in a reclaimed industrial facility. The six-course dinner menu (without wine) is 600 kroner.

## 4 **RELÆ**

Jægersborggade 41
Copenhagen N ④
+45 3696 6609
*www.restaurant-relae.dk*

Located on one of the hippest streets in Copenhagen, Relæ never announces their 'menu of the day' early, you just have to show up to find out what's for dinner. Four-course dinner for 450 kroner (without wine).

## 5 **PONY**

Vesterbrogade 135
Copenhagen V ③
+45 3322 1000
*www.ponykbh.dk*

This chic neighbourhood bistro is the casual 'little brother' of the exclusive Michelin-starred restaurant Kadeau. The menu still offers a fantastic selection of New Nordic cuisine inspired, in large part, by the produce coming from the Danish island of Bornholm. Expect dinner and wine for around 300 kroner.

# 5

# CLASSIC DANISH

## *dishes worth trying*

---

### 6   SMØRREBRØD

Translated literally as 'butter bread,' 'smørrebrød' is a broad term referring to a wide spectrum of Danish open-faced sandwiches served on dark, dense rye bread. Smørrebrød is typically topped with some combination of cold meats, fish, vegetables, cheese, and, of course, butter. You can find specialty shops all over the city that prepare fresh smørrebrød daily.

### 7   FLØDEBOLLER

Dark chocolate, marzipan, marshmallow cream – what's not to love? These classic Danish sweets are often served on top of ice cream, but are also delicious on their own. The best can be found in Copenhagen's many chocolate shops or artisanal bakeries.

8 **GAMMEL DANSK**

Made from a secret recipe of 29 herbs, spices, and flowers, Gammel Dansk is a pungent spirit often enjoyed on special occasions. Love it or hate it, but taste it at least once.

9 **DANISH HOT DOG**

Wrapped in bacon, topped with fried onions, sweet pickles, and your choice of sweet ketchup or spicy mustard, this is the ultimate Copenhagen street food. Look for *pølsevogns* (sausage wagons) throughout the capital.

10 **FLÆSKESTEG**

A slow roasted pork roast served with crispy pork cracklings, warm pickled red cabbage, and caramelized potatoes, *flæskesteg* is the classic Danish comfort food.

6 SMØRREBRØD

## *5 places to sample*
# DANISH SMØRREBRØD

11 **TOLD & SNAPS**
   Toldbodgade 2
   Copenhagen K ①
   +45 3393 8385
   *www.toldogsnaps.dk*

Since 2000, the chefs at Told & Snaps have been serving high quality smørrebrød topped with your choice of the essentials: pickled herring, liver pate, roast beef, and/or salmon. Also, don't miss their extensive menu of flavoured *snaps*, the 'blackcurrant, wild liquorice and star aniseed' is recommended.

12 **AAMANNS DELI**
   Øster Farimagsgade 10
   Copenhagen Ø ⑤
   +45 3555 3344
   *www.aamanns.dk*

Since 2006, chef Adam Aamann's deli has offered some of the capital's best open faced sandwiches for in-shop dining and as takeaway. With a focus on creativity and seasonal ingredients, Aamanns brings a refreshingly modern sensibility to the smørrebrød tradition.

13 **SCHØNNEMANN**
   Hauser Plads 16
   Copenhagen K ①
   +45 3312 0785
   *www.restaurant
   schonnemann.dk*

Schønnemann is Copenhagen's quintessential, old-school Danish smørrebrød restaurant. With its dark wood interior, white table-cloths, and classic seafood-centric menu, this lunch only establishment has been serving up the classics since 1877.

## 14 LUMSKEBUGTEN

Esplanaden 21
Copenhagen K ⓘ
+45 3315 6029
*www.lumskebugten.dk*

This elegant restaurant has a long and storied past, having served for years as a sailor's tavern, dating back to 1854. Today, Lumskebugten (treacherous bay) is an elegant restaurant serving Danish cuisine, of which smørrebrød is a specialty. If you feel like splurging on lunch, try the three-course menu.

## 15 HALLERNES SMØRREBRØD

Torvehallerne Hall 1
Rømersgade 21
Copenhagen K ⓘ
+45 6070 4780
*www.hallernes.dk*

For a simpler, more vibrant smørrebrød experience, head to the Torvehallerne food market. Here, Hallernes Smørrebrød serves fresh, creative open-face sandwiches made right in front of you. Hallernes also offers the advantage of being open later than most other smørrebrød spots in town.

12 AAMANNS DELI

# *The 5 best*
# BAKERIES

16 **MEYERS BAGERI**
**Jægersborggade 9**
**Copenhagen N** ④
**+45 2510 1134**

Meyers Bageri is the small chain of organic, artisanal bread and pastry shops scattered throughout Copenhagen that originate with Claus Meyer, one of Denmark's culinary superstars. But rather than succumbing to rapid over-commercialization, the Meyers bakeries have stayed small, local, and committed to quality.

17 **BAGERIET BRØD**
**Enghave Plads 7**
**Copenhagen V** ③
**+45 3322 8007**

Trendy Vesterbro's hippest organic bakery is only a few years old but already feels like an essential part of the neighbour-hood. Brød's lovingly crafted rustic breads are highly recommended.

18 **SANKT PEDERS BAGERI**
**Skt Peders Stræde 29**
**Copenhagen K** ①
**+45 3311 1129**

Sankt Peders Bageri is a relatively low-key place with a traditional vibe. But what makes this bakery so special is their beloved *Onsdag sneglen* (Wednesday cinnamon rolls), of which they bake 4000 each week. Tip: arrive early and buy two.

### 19 BØJES BRØD

**Ordrupvej 101**
**Charlottenlund** ⑧
**+45 3513 6000**
*www.bøjesbrød.dk*

The people at Bøjes Brød love baking, eating, and sharing their outstanding baked goods – this becomes clear as soon as you enter the cheerful, stylish bakery in the little village of Ordrup. This award-winning bakery is a worthwhile detour en route from the city centre to Bellevue Beach or Dyrehaven.

### 20 MIRABELLE

**Guldbergsgade 29**
**Copenhagen N** ④
**+45 3535 4724**

A self described 'bakery and diner,' Mirabelle was opened by former Noma chef Christian Puglisi. What makes Mirabelle so special is the fact that this bakery is open later, you can actually dine in and enjoy the bakery's cosy Scandinavian interiors. Tip: try the marzipan cake.

19 BØJES BRØD

# *The 5 best restaurants for*
# COPENHAGEN ATMOSPHERE

---

### 21 MANFREDS & VIN
**Jægersborggade 40**
**Copenhagen N** ④
**+45 3696 65930**
*www.manfreds.dk*

In the spirit of Parisian *bobo* (at once bourgeois and bohemian), Manfreds & Vin brings a serious Nordic sensibility to trendy Jægersborggade. With its extensive lists of wines and healthy meals, Manfreds never disappoints. Recommended: the house's Kolster beer and the 'chef's selection' seven-plate lunch.

### 22 ALMANAK AT THE STANDARD
**Havnegade 4**
**Copenhagen K** ①
**+45 7214 8808**
*www.thestandardcph.dk*

Almanak is the essential Copenhagen restaurant: elegant, modern interiors, waterfront views, and outstanding Nordic-centric food. On top of that, Almanak is located inside 'The Standard', one of Copenhagen's most iconic buildings. Tip: book a table for lunch when the views are better and the prices are lower.

22 ALMANAK AT THE STANDARD

### 23 UNION KITCHEN

Store Strandstræde 21
Copenhagen K ①
+45 3314 5488
*www.theunionkitchen.dk*

Just a street away from the tourist crowds of Nyhavn, this funky urban diner combines much of what makes Copenhagen so cool: a laidback attitude but with a serious attention to the details – both in the restaurant's rustic interiors and unique menu offerings. Recommended: the 'Kitchen Chicken and Waffles.'

### 24 ATELIER SEPTEMBER

Gothersgade 30
Copenhagen K ①
+45 2629 5753
*www.atelierseptember.dk*

With window views onto busy Gothersgade and minimal, rustic interiors, Atelier September is rich with Copenhagen atmosphere from the outside looking in and vice versa. Monday through Saturday this spot is a favorite among the Copenhagen chic for coffee and light meals.

### 25 MADKLUBBEN BISTRO-DE-LUXE

Store Kongensgade 66
Copenhagen K ①
+45 3332 3234
*www.madklubben.dk/
bistro-de-luxe*

The Madklubben family of restaurants scattered around Copenhagen are each aesthetically distinct but what unites them all is their commitment to serving creative, quality food at a fair price. Bistro-de-Luxe on Store Kongensgade is the original Madklubben and offers a unique Copenhagen experience.

## The 5 best places to
# EAT NEAR
# THE STRØGET

---

26 **BARBURRITO**
Gothersgade 27
Copenhagen K ⓘ
*www.barburrito.dk*

Burburrito serves up Mexican favorites
with a minimal, New Nordic twist. The
burritos here are their specialty – the
confit pork is recommended, but for the
ultimate meal, make sure to add a side
of plantain chips and guacamole and a
handmade jalepeño-infused margarita.

27 **LANTERNE ROUGE**
Kompagnistræde 16
Copenhagen K ⓘ
+45 7211 8199
*www.lanternerouge.dk*

This modern, rustic bistro does it all:
quality food and drinks, an inviting
atmosphere, and a really friendly staff.
Order the fantastic *moules frites* (or the
steak frites) and enjoy people watching
from the front windows or terrace.

28 **PALUDAN BOOK & CAFE**
Fiolstræde 10-12
Copenhagen K ⓘ
+45 3315 0675
*www.paludan-cafe.dk*

You may have to fight off the crowds of
university students to secure a table at
Paludan, but your struggle will be worth
it. Giant sandwiches, fresh pastries,
excellent coffees and all at traveller-
friendly prices. Before you leave,
make sure to explore the secondhand
bookstore in the cafe's basement.

## 29  CAFÉ SKILDPADDEN

Gråbrødretorv 9
Copenhagen K ①
+45 3313 05069
*www.skildpadden.dk*

*Skildpadden* is Danish for 'the turtle' and this candle-lit cafe and sandwich bar, tucked away in the beautifully hidden Gråbrødretorv square, is indeed a great place to slow down and enjoy a meal, a game of backgammon, or the cafe's free Wi-Fi.

## 30  PASTIS

Gothersgade 52
Copenhagen K ①
+45 3393 4411
*www.bistro-pastis.dk*

This bistro combines stylish Danish dining with classic French cuisine. Pastis' lunch menu is excellent (and less expensive than dinner); the Niçoise salad and *boeuf rôti* sandwich are two of the best meals in town. Recommended: a glass of house red wine with lunch and a cup of locally-roasted Kontra coffee afterwards.

27 LANTERNE ROUGE

# 5 *essential*
# FOOD TRUCKS
# AT PAPER ISLAND

Copenhagen Street Food
Trangravsvej 14
Christianshavn ②

31 **OINK OINK BARBECUE**
*www.oinkoink.dk*

It is usually a good sign when a food truck has a small menu, where a limited number of items means the house has a more focused specialty. This is certainly the case at Oink Oink, whose famous slow roasted pulled pork 'burger' is the undisputed star of the show.

32 **COPPER & WHEAT**
*www.copperandwheat.com*

The five most important words you need to know about Copper & Wheat are: double fried duck fat fries. And although the two French guys, Alex and Pierre, change up their menu options every week, Copenhagen's most epic fries are always on the menu.

33 **BULKO**
+45 2971 2580
*www.bulko.dk*

Bulko stands for authentic South Korean BBQ with a modern, youthful twist. Chef Oliver Ko has brought the best of Seoul street cuisine to the Copenhagen dining scene.

## 34 TACOS CHUCHO

As a rule, it's not easy to find authentic Mexican food in Copenhagen, but Tacos Chucho are definitely the exception to that rule. From his silver camper on Paper Island, chef Mario Alberto Cruz is churning out the city's freshest tacos, made with colourful, locally sourced ingredients.

## 35 BRASA

Brazilians are known around the world as masters of gourmet grilled meat, and this reputation is proudly reinforced at the Brasa food truck at Paper Island, where visitors are treated to a plate of three meats (marinated for 24 hours each) slow cooked over a charcoal fire and flavoured to perfection.

34 TACOS CHUCHO

# *The 5 best*
# VEGETARIAN
## *restaurants*

---

### 36   SIMPLERAW

**Oehlenschlægersgade 12**
**Copenhagen** V ③
**+45 3535 3005**
*www.simpleraw.dk*

Even if you're not a vegetarian, simpleRAW is worth a visit. Located on one of the coolest streets in Vesterbro, simpleRAW has something for everyone: incredible juices, truly creative raw food options, and an interesting 'raw timber' interior design that complements the menu. Recommended: the quinoa burger with apple ginger dressing.

### 37   42RAW

**Pilestræde 32**
**Copenhagen** K ①
**+45 3212 3210**
*www.42raw.dk*

42Raw is an entirely vegan, up-and-coming chain of raw food eateries in and around Copenhagen, which means there are several locations to choose from. 42Raw specializes in fresh, sustainable food that is prepared in a dehydrator (not an oven) and never heated above 42 degrees celsius (hence the name).

## 38  **MORGENSTEDET**
Fabriksområdet 134
Christiania
Christianshavn ②
*www.morgenstedet.dk*

For over two decades, the cosy, volunteer-run Morgenstedet 'dining club' has been one of Copenhagen's best vegetarian restaurants. Hidden away in the independent commune of Christiania, both the chefs and the menu at Morgenstedet rotate daily, which creates a lot of culinary creativity and diversity from day to day. Closed on Mondays.

## 39  **CAFÉ N**
Blågårdsgade 17
Copenhagen N ④
+45 3215 6852
*www.cafe-n-2200.dk*

This tiny cafe has a simple mission: to provide 'vegetarian delights and living comfort at prices everyone can afford'. And Café N, located on trendy Blågårdsgade, is successfully fulfilling its mission: at only 99 kroner, the 'Vegan Brunch' is one of Copenhagen's best: tofu omelet, hummus, tzatziki, croquettes, fruit, salad and bread.

## 40  **BIOM**
Fredericiagade 78
Copenhagen K ①
+45 3332 2466
*www.biom.dk*

Modern, organic, and gourmet are the three best adjectives to describe Biom, Copenhagen's popular vegetarian-friendly eco-eatery. Serving outstanding lunch, brunch, and dinner, Biom's staff shows off its food prep in an open kitchen and loves to educate diners on the stories behind their sustainable ingredients and dishes. Recommended: the daily lunch platter.

# The 5 best
# SEAFOOD
## restaurants

---

### 41 OYSTERS & GRILL
Sjællandsgade 1B
Copenhagen N ④
+45 7020 61716

Laidback, funky, and vibrant, dining at Oysters & Grill feels like visiting a seaside bistro that has been imported from somewhere along the Mediterranean. Book a table ahead because, even mid-week, this place can be packed with happy, oyster-guzzling diners.

### 42 FISKERIKAJEN AT TORVEHALLERNE
Frederiksborggade 21
Copenhagen K ①
+45 2680 7067
*www.fiskerikajen.dk*

Located inside the Torvehallerne food market, Fiskerikajen serves up the city's best fish tacos: made with freshly caught fish, pickled red cabbage, and chili mayo. Tacos not your thing? Don't worry: Fiskerikajen also makes an expert version of fish and chips.

### 43 KROGS FISKERESTAURANT
Gammel Strand 38
Copenhagen K ①
+45 3315 8915
*www.krogs.dk*

This posh, canalside restaurant has been serving fresh Nordic fish since 1910. Recently, Krogs has reinvented itself with a new focus on innovation and experimentation, adding yet another chapter to the story of one of Copenhagen's most beloved institutions.

## 44 PASTIS FISHMARKET

**Hovedvagtsgade 2**
**Copenhagen K** ①
**+45 8816 9999**
*www.fishmarket.dk*

Pastis Fishmarket is the new, seafood-focused sibling of Pastis, Copenhagen's best French-style bistro. And like the original Pastis, Fishmarket does food, atmosphere, and service with stylish excellence. And don't skip dessert – Fishmarket does all the French classics.

## 45 FISKEBAREN

**Flæsketorvet 100**
**Copenhagen V** ③
**+45 3215 5656**
*www.fiskebaren.dk*

There seems to be no end to the praise for Fiskebaren; everyone from *The New York Times* to the BBC has featured this restaurant for both its exceptional Nordic cuisine and its impressive industrial chic ambiance. Recommended: the blue mussels in apple cider and the house's New Nordic version of fish and chips.

45 FISKEBAREN

# 5 must-try Danish
# LIQUORICE
## *treats*

---

### 46  SOCIAL FOODIES
Østerbrogade 128
Copenhagen Ø ⑤
+45 2210 0136
*www.socialfoodies.dk*

The only treat that Danes love more than liquorice is ice cream, so it makes perfect sense that most (if not all) Copenhagen ice cream shops combine these two delicious passions. And while many different shops have some variation of liquorice ice cream (liquorice and chocolate, liquorice and salt, etc.), the sustainability-minded Social Foodies serves up the best.

### 47  LAKRIDS
BY JOHAN BÜLOW
Torvehallerne Market
Frederiksborggade 21
Copenhagen K ①
*www.liquorice.nu*

Since 2007, LAKRIDS by Johan Bülow has been thé name when it comes to gourmet liquorice treats coming out of Denmark: from organic liquorice candies to raw liquorice cooking ingredients. If you're already a liquorice lover, try LAKRIDS' No.5 Salty Chili Cranberry Liquorice. But if you're still a sceptic, then start with LAKRIDS' A Chocolate Coated Liquorice.

## 48 ØSTERSØ COLA

**Lidkoeb Cocktail Bar**
**Vesterbrogade 72B**
**Copenhagen V ③**
**+45 3311 2010**
*www.lidkoeb.dk*

One of the most creative cocktails from one of Copenhagen's hippest bars, Lidkoeb's fantastic Østersø Cola is made from Pimm's No.1, Ketel One Vodka, peach, lemon juice and sweet raw liquorice syrup.

## 49 LIQUORICE STOUT BEER

Lots of microbreweries in Copenhagen are brewing up beers infused with liquorice these days. If you're lucky, Mikkeller Bar in Vesterbro will have one on tap during your visit. Otherwise, pick up a bottle of Svaneke Bryghus Liquorice Stout.

## 50 EARTH CONTROL BRAND SALTY LICORICE CRISPS

COPENHAGEN AREA SHOPS

Technically these crisps are a Finnish product, but they are available in almost all the grocery stores in and around Copenhagen. Liquorice and potato somehow work well together in this quirky, salty snack. An ideal pair with a golden or amber ale.

47 LAKRIDS

## *The 5 most overlooked*
# HIDDEN GEMS

---

51 **MA'ED ETHIOPIAN RESTAURANT**
Griffenfeldsgade 7
Copenhagen N ④
+45 3184 24538
*www.maed.dk*

Locals who have been to Ma'ed once, always go back again, and again. The cafe's interiors are humble but their wonderfully exotic food is some of the most delicious, affordable, and filling in Copenhagen.

52 **COSTA SMERALDA**
Strandvejen 323
Charlottenlund ⑧
+45 3964 3202
*www.costasmeralda.dk*

Regularly voted as one of Denmark's best pizza shops, the guys at Costa Smeralda do all of the classic Italian favourites with passion and precision. Since 1989, this seaside pizzeria has been an essential, year-round destination for locals. Ask about the 'pizza of the month' and then order one.

53 **IL BUCO**
Njalsgade 19C
Copenhagen S ⑦
*www.ilbuco.dk*

The low-lit atmosphere and the owners' attention to detail make every trip to the uber cosy Il Buco memorable. Every Tuesday night Il Buco hosts its popular 'dinner club', a generous gourmet Italian meal (six courses and a glass of wine) at a special low price. Book ahead, reservation required.

## 54  CHRISTIANSHAVNS FÆRGECAFÉ
**Strandgade 50**
**Christianshavn** ②
**+45 3254 46249**
*www.faergecafeen.dk*

First established in the 18th century, the lovely 'ferry cafe' is located right beside the scenic Amsterdam-inspired canal waters of Christianshavn and serves excellent Danish cuisine and homemade aquavit.

## 55  VESPA
**Store Kongensgade 90**
**Copenhagen K** ①
**+45 3311 3700**

Vespa is a New Nordic take on all your favorites from Italy. The house menu changes at least once a month, but the best bet is to order the set, four-course menu, which is always surprising and filling (for less than 300 kroner).

53 IL BUCO

# *The 5 most authentic*
# DANISH-STYLE
# HOT DOGS

---

56 **JOHN'S HOTDOG DELI**
**Bernstorffsgade**
**Copenhagen K** ①
**+45 3132 5848**

Located directly in front of the Copenhagen's central train station and across the street from Tivoli Gardens, John's Deli is also a kind of local landmark, taking the already intricate art of Danish hot dogs to a whole new level with his homemade sauces and thoughtfully sourced meat.

57 **HARRY'S PLACE**
**Nordre Fasanvej 269**
**Copenhagen N** ④
**+45 2015 1960**
*www.harrysplace.dk*

For over 50 years, Harry's Place has been serving the classic Copenhagen-style hot dogs to commuters, workers, and at least two Danish prime ministers. The highlight of their menu is the large 'Børge' sausage, which locals say is best enjoyed with Harry's special 'gunpowder sauce' and a glass of chocolate milk.

58 **PØLSE KOMPAGNIET**
**Gothersgade 154 St Tv**
**Copenhagen K** ①
**+45 4274 7247**
*www.polsekompagniet.dk*

By combining fresh baked bread, homemade dips, and organic sausage recipes inspired by French, Moroccan, and Italian traditions, Pølse Kompagniet (the sausage company) is Copenhagen's premier gourmet hot dog wagon.

## 59 DEN ØKOLOGISKE PØLSEMAND

**Amagertorv 31**
**Copenhagen K** ①
**+45 3020 4025**
*www.doep.dk*

Known by locals as DØP, this award-winning eatery has distinguished itself as a new kind of Danish hot dog wagon, serving food made exclusively with 100% organic ingredients. Find DØP hot dog wagons near The Round Tower and Helligaandskirken (Church of the Holy Spirit).

## 60 NYHAVN PØLSEVOGNS

NEAR KONGENS NYTORV
METRO STATION
**Copenhagen K** ①

One of the most picturesque views of Copenhagen is certainly the colourful buildings, boats, and bicycles of Nyhavn. But along with the historic architecture and tourist bars, Nyhavn is also home to several quality *pølsevogns* (sausage wagons). At Nyhavn, they all make delicious hot dogs, so you can't go wrong. Just remember to enjoy the view as well.

59 DEN ØKOLOGISKE PØLSEMAND

# *The 5 best*
# **ASIAN** *restaurants*

---

**61  LÊLÊ STREET KITCHEN**
Østerbrogade 56
Copenhagen Ø ⑤
+45 5373 7345
*www.lele.dk*

Originally established as a single Vietnamese takeaway shop, the award-winning LêLê eateries are now popping up all around the city – and for good reason. On Østerbrogade, you can dine in or take away the Lê family's amazing homemade food for a picnic along the Østerbro lakes, just across the street.

**62  AROII**
Guldbergsgade 23
Copenhagen N ④
+45 3535 9505
*www.aroii.dk*

With three locations in Copenhagen (and more on the way), Aroii is quickly staking a claim as Copenhagen's most popular family of Asian bistros. Originally started as the little brother of the Michelin-starred (and pricey) restaurant Kiin Kiin, Aroii does everything well. Recommended: the house's famous Red Curry.

### 63 CAFÉ LOPPEN

Sydområdet 4e
Christiania
Christianshavn ②
+45 4118 41165
*www.cafeloppen.com*

Café Loppen is yet another of Copenhagen's best kept secrets that can be found tucked away in the Freetown of Christiania. Specializing in Thai delicacies, Café Loppen serves straightforward, flavourful dishes in a historic and unique atmosphere.

### 64 NAMNAM

Vesterbrogade 39
Copenhagen V ③
+45 4191 9898
*www.restaurant namnam.dk*

Drawing on the best from Chinese, Singaporean, and Indonesian cuisine, the menu at namnam is officially categorized as 'Peranakan'. And with celebrity chef Claus Meyer as one of the owners, you can trust that all of the food will be made with creativity and expertise.

### 65 GREEN MANGO

Torvegade 16
Copenhagen K ①
+45 2811 4000
*www.greenmango.dk*

This inexpensive fresh takeaway shop isn't an especially 'cool' urban eatery, but Green Mango does delicious, reliable, and – if you prefer – very spicy Thai food takeaway with excellence.

64 NAMNAM

# *The 5 best meals in the*
# MEATPACKING
# DISTRICT

---

### 66 HIJA DE SANCHEZ

**Slagterboderne 8**
**Copenhagen V ③**
**+45 3118 5203**
*www.hijadesanchez.dk*

Opened in 2016, Hija De Sanchez has filled a gaping hole in Copenhagen's foodie scene where, until now, high-quality 'fresh-Mex' has been non existent. Opened by Noma-trained, Mexican-American chef Rosio Sanchez, this *tacquería* (taco stand) deserves all the loving hype it receives. You won't find more authentic Mexican cuisine anywhere in the capital.

### 67 KUL

**Høkerboderne 16B-20**
**Copenhagen V ③**
**+45 3321 0033**
*www.restaurantkul.dk*

The menu at Kul is an international celebration of all things cooked on the grill. One of the higher-end restaurants in the Kødbyen, Kul is led by two Michelin-starred chefs who offer up a fantastic variety of menu options ranging from Singaporean spareribs to lobster salad to *jamón ibérico*.

68 **BIOMIO**
Halmtorvet 19
Copenhagen V ③
+45 3331 2000
*www.biomio.dk*

Copenhagen is one of the greenest cities in the world and BioMio is Copenhagen's greenest restaurant: featuring sustainably sourced wood tables, energy saving lights, eco-friendly cocktails, and an entirely organic menu of vegetable-centric dishes. Best of all, the food here is incredible. Tip: go for lunch and beat the crowds.

69 **MOTHER**
Høkerboderne 9-15
Copenhagen V ③
+45 2227 5898
*www.mother.dk*

Founded by a Roman emigré to Copenhagen, Mother does pizza the way it is supposed to be done: with fresh ingredients, a Neapolitan crust, and cooked in an wood-fired oven. No wonder Copenhageners line up around the block for this pizza – no question, the best in town. Tip: try Mother's unique brunch on the weekends from 11 am till 3 pm.

70 **GORILLA**
Flæsketorvet 57
Copenhagen V ③
+45 3333 8330
*www.restaurantgorilla.dk*

The eclectic menu at Gorilla borrows the best elements from various world cuisines, including (but not limited to) Asian, South American, and New Nordic favourites. For the ultimate foodie experience, order Gorilla's 10 or 15 plate snack servings for the whole table.

68 BIOMIO

# The 5 best places for
# KEBAB/SHAWARMA

―――――――

71 **AHAAA**
**Blågårdsgade 21**
**Copenhagen N** ④
**+45 3539 0085**
*www.ahaaa.dk*

The Nørrebro district of Copenhagen is the city's epicenter for Middle Eastern cuisine. And one of the best all-around spots for fresh ingredients, generous portions, and good vibes is Ahaaa, located along the artsy walking street Blågårdsgade. Recommended: any large plate, enjoyed at one of the cafe's outdoor tables.

72 **LIBAN CUISINE**
**Rantzausgade 1**
**Copenhagen N** ④
**+45 3811 5050**

The brightly coloured Lebanese dishes at Liban are refreshingly diverse when compared to many similar style eateries. Much of Liban's menu is vegetarian friendly, but don't worry carnivores – Liban also does excellent shawarma and burgers for dine in or take away.

## 73 KEBABISTAN

Istedgade 105
Copenhagen V ③
+45 3322 8993

There are a few Kebabistan shops in Copenhagen and all of them are popular with locals, both day and night. Don't plan on 'dining in' here – this is proper takeaway street food and you'll likely have to queue (which is always a good sign, right?). Recommended: go for the shawarma or falafel on fresh bread.

## 74 LA CENTRALE

Nørrebrogade 31
Copenhagen N ④
www.lacentrale-2200.dk

This family-run shop is located on Nørrebro's busy main street, where customers are picky and competition is fierce among the numerous Middle Eastern eateries. But Mahir and the team of La Centrale have proven they are here to stay. Recommended: the baked aubergine and any of the house's large plates.

## 75 PASHA KEBAB

Enghavevej 57
Copenhagen N ④
+45 3918 1122
www.pasha-kebab.dk

Don't let the neon lights scare you away from Pasha Kebab, this place is the real thing. Beloved by locals, Pasha cooks a lot of their dishes right over a charcoal fire making their meats exceptionally flavourful and, frankly, addictive. Tip: the #27 and #30 are amazing.

# The 5 best
# BURGER BARS

---

76 **TOMMI'S BURGER JOINT**
Høkerboderne 19-23
Copenhagen V ③
+45 3514 4421
*www.burgerjoint.dk*

There's no cooler place to eat burgers in Copenhagen than Tommi's. Located in the newly revived Meatpacking District, Tommi's serves straightforward American style burgers (the buns here are incredible) with chips and a soft drink for less than 100 kroner. As you can imagine, locals adore this place.

77 **GRILLEN**
Nørrebrogade 13
Copenhagen N ④
+45 3535 3569
*www.grillenburgerbar.dk*

At the east end of colourful Nørrebrogade, Grillen is one of the city's fastest growing burger sensations. With their high-quality food, stylish interiors, and rock-bottom prices, it's easy to see how Grillen is becoming an addiction for many locals.

78 **GASOLINE GRILL**
Landgreven 10
Copenhagen K ①
*www.facebook.com/
gasolinegrill*

Copenhagen's newest burger obsession housed in an old petrol station. With organic ingredients, fair prices, friendly staff, and creative 'burgers of the day', it's no wonder that even the staff from Noma come here to satisfy their burger cravings.

## 79 SPORVEJEN

Gråbrødretorv 17
Copenhagen K ①
+45 3313 3101
*www.sporvejen.dk*

There is nowhere else in town quite like Sporvejen – a burger bar built inside one of Copenhagen's historic electric tram cars. But don't be distracted by the thematic kitsch of the interiors; the burgers here are authentic, massive, and inexpensive.

## 80 FISCH-ART AT COPEN-HAGEN STREET FOOD

(PAPER ISLAND)
Trangravsvej 14
Christianshavn ②
+49 160 2001512

The German couple who run Fisch-Art are making some of Copenhagen's most creative and mouthwatering burgers. Highly recommended is the towering 'Surf & Turf Burger' – a beef burger topped with whisky-marinated onions, bacon, grilled shrimp, and served on homemade sourdough bread.

76 TOMMI'S BURGER JOINT

# 5 must-visit
# STALLS AT THE TORVEHALLERNE

Torvehallerne
Frederiksborggade 21
Copenhagen K ①

81 **MA POULE**
+45 2763 1981

With their selection of cheeses, pate, foie gras, and wines, Ma Poule brings the French market experience to Copenhagen. The team that runs the shop are authentically French and a lot of fun to banter with. Ma Poule's curry duck confit sandwich is often voted as one of Copenhagen's best.

82 **STIGS OLIVEN**

Whether you're interested in artisanal olive oils, high quality spice mixes, or just curious to taste a spectrum of olive varieties, Stigs Olives has a lot to offer. The shopkeeper will let you taste everything until you find your favourite.

83 **SUMMERBIRD CHOCOLATE**
+45 3314 8148
*www.summerbird.dk*

This organic chocolate shop does a lot of sweet treats really well, but their specialty is Danish *flødebolle* – rich dark chocolate bells filled with sweet marshmallow cream and marzipan.

## 84 GRANNYS HOUSE
*www.grannyshouse.dk*

There are a lot of great bakeries in Copenhagen, from the fashionable to the old-fashioned, and the idiosyncratic Grannys House falls somewhere in the middle. The staff are friendly, the decor is kitschy, but, the bottom line is that the breads are excellent.

## 85 NOORBOHANDELEN
+45 5178 0448
*www.noorbohandelen.dk*

You choose the bottle, you choose your favourite liqueur or spirit, and let the team at Noorbohandelen take it from there. This truly unique drinks shop offers a wide range of small-batch and limited edition alcoholic specialties to sample, select and take home. The shop's customized bottles also make for beautiful gifts and souvenirs.

TORVEHALLERNE

## The 5 best places for a
# CHEAP QUALITY MEAL

86 **GRØD**
Jægersborggade 50
Copenhagen N ④
+45 5058 5579
*www.groed.com*

Grød is Copenhagen's most popular destination for warm, delicious, healthy, and inexpensive comfort food. In true Copenhagen style, the team at Grød have transformed porridge-making into an art form. Recommended: the savory *bygotto* with artichokes, fresh thyme, and ricotta cheese.

86 GRØD

## 87 ABSALON CPH

Sønder Blvd. 73
Copenhagen V ③
*www.absaloncph.dk*

Eating out is never cheap in Copenhagen, but there are some places doing delicious and affordable food. One of the most creative of these is Absalon CPH, a church that has been converted into a community center. Absalon hosts a variety of fun nightly events and serves an amazing dinner every night (for only 50 kroner).

## 88 CAFÉ CADEAU

H.C. Ørsteds Vej 28
Frederiksberg ⑥
+45 3326 2028
*www.cafecadeau.dk*

Run entirely by volunteers, Café Cadeau is a non-profit cafe that serves quality homemade food at a very good price. Cadeau's internationally-themed 'dish of the day' changes each day but is always a delicious surprise. Also open for weekend brunch.

## 89 UN MERCATO

Torvehallerne
Frederiksborggade 21
Copenhagen K ①
+45 5114 4466

The lunch special at Un Mercato is incredible: an artisanal sandwich, fresh rosemary fries, and a glass of wine for only 115 kroner. If you feel like splurging a little, add an order of the heavenly lamb and saffron risotto balls.

## 90 SLICE OF COPENHAGEN

Sværtegade 3
Copenhagen K ①
+45 3391 2002
*www.sliceofcopenhagen.dk*

Offering a range of creative sandwiches and pizzas by the slice, this central spot rises above the numerous other pizza shops in town. Recommended: the Spanish chorizo slice.

# *The 5 best places for*
# SWEET TREATS

---

**91  CONDITORIET LA GLACE**
Skoubogade 3
Copenhagen K ①
+45 3314 4646,
*www.laglace.dk*

For nearly 150 years, Conditoriet La Glace has been crafting Copenhagen's most exquisite wedding cakes, pastries, and colourful sweet treats. Rich with tradition and old world charm, enjoying a coffee and cake at Conditoriet La Glace is a little like (high calorie) time travelling.

**92  BERTELS KAGER**
Falkoner Allé 54
Frederiksberg ⑥
+45 3313 0033
*www.bertelskager.dk*

With over 100 different recipes in their repertoire (many rotate with the season's ingredients), Bertels cheesecake shop will certainly have something for every kind of sweet tooth. And, if your cake craving hits you after dinner, you're in luck: this award-winning cakery is open late most nights.

**93  PETER BEIER CHOKOLADE**
Nordre Frihavnsgade 20
Copenhagen Ø ⑤
+45 3538 0110
*www.pbchokolade.dk*

Since 1996, Peter Beier has been thé name in artisanal Danish chocolate goodies. And luckily for visitors to Copenhagen, Peter Beier's ethically sourced and sustainably produced delicacies are now available in boutique locations throughout the capital.

## 94 NAMNAM SLIK
**Amagerbrogade 72**
**Copenhagen S** ⑦
**+45 3296 6071**

Denmark is a nation with a huge appetite for colourful, wonderful, tooth-rotting candy. And NamNam Slik is one of the best local shops for indulging in the love of chocolates, gummies, and other treats. Tip: Friday is officially candy day in Copenhagen, so why not join the tradition by filling up a bag of *fredags slik* (Friday candy).

## 95 THE DONUT SHOP
**Jægersborggade 5**
**Copenhagen N** ④
**+45 2629 7918**
*www.thedonutshop.dk*

Although the shop's flavours rotate daily, there is always something to love on their menu. Recommended: the 'coco loco' and the 'marzipan caramel fudge'.

91 **CONDITORIET LA GLACE**

# The 5 best spots for
# SUNDAY BRUNCH

---

**96  CAFÉ JORDEN RUNDT**
Strandvejen 152
Charlottenlund ⑧
+45 3963 7381
*www.cafejordenrundt.dk*

Located along Strandvejen – Copenhagen's scenic coastal road – this circular, all-glass cafe is busy every day, but especially on sunny Sundays, when groups of cyclists gather for post-ride meals and drinks outside on the terrace. But even under cloudy, rainy skies, Jorden Rundt is a classic destination for Sunday brunch.

**97  RESTAURANT CHARLOTTENLUND FORT**
Strandvejen 150
Charlottenlund ⑧
+45 3962 2263
*www.charlottenlund fortet.dk*

With waterfront views toward Sweden, the affordable brunch at Charlottenlund Fort is served buffet-style and every detail is perfect. Make sure to book a table ahead of time.

**98  WULF & KONSTALI FOOD SHOP**
Lergravsvej 57
Copenhagen S ⑦
+45 3254 8181
*www.wogk.dk*

Known as 'the most photographed brunch in Copenhagen' Wulf & Konstali's reputation is well-deserved. With their build your own-style brunch, stylish interiors, and excellent bakery/coffee shop, this place does it all well.

## 99 KALASET

**Vendersgade 16**
**Copenhagen K** ①
**+45 3333 0035**
*www.kalaset.dk*

The name of this eclectic, centrally located cafe means 'the party' in Swedish and, on weekends, this place is packed with hungry 'partygoers'. This local, partially underground cafe is known for it's friendly, neighbourhood vibe and vegetarian menu options.

## 100 CAFE HØEGS

**Enghavevej 20**
**Copenhagen V** ③
**+45 3331 3489**
*www.hoegs.dk*

Nestled at the edge of the bustling districts of Vesterbro and Frederiksberg, the funky Cafe Høegs has something for everyone. With a solid drinks menu and a proven reputation in the neighbourhood for great food, this is an ideal spot to take in a long, indulgent weekend brunch, especially when the sun is out.

98 WULF & KONSTALI

BANG & JENSEN

# 60 PLACES
# FOR A DRINK

# *The 5 best*
# DANISH
# MICROBREWERIES

---

### 101 NØRREBRO BRYGHUS
**Ryesgade 3**
**Copenhagen N** ④
**+45 3530 0530**
*www.noerrebrobryghus.dk*

This celebrated craft brewery has been around since 2003 and has brewed over 200 different beers since their inception, inspired by American, German, and Belgian traditions. Tip: book a table in the Nørrebro Bryghus restaurant balcony and enjoy watching the brewery in action.

### 102 MIKKELLER BAR
**Viktoriagade 8 B-C**
**Copenhagen V** ③
**+45 3331 0415**
*www.mikkeller.dk*

Mikkeller is the current darling of the Copenhagen craft brew scene. Although founder Mikkel Borg Bjergsø's creations are now being exported to over 30 countries, the beermaker continues to challenge convention and delight patrons with innovative and surprising beers.

### 103 BREWPUB
**Vestergade 29**
**Copenhagen K** ①
**+45 3332 0060**
*www.brewpub.dk*

Central, refined, and bustling, BrewPub has seven custom brews on tap every day, along with seven 'guest beers' from other Danish microbreweries. If the weather allows it, make sure to take advantage of BrewPub's gorgeous beer garden.

## 104 WARPIGS

**Flæsketorvet 25-37**
**Copenhagen V** ③
*www.warpigs.dk*

A new Texas-style BBQ restaurant and microbrewery. The result of a collaboration between Mikkeller and US brewery 3Floyds, Warpigs offers beer lovers a diverse selection of house beers that pair perfectly with the house's specialty smoked meats.

## 105 ØLSNEDKEREN

**Griffenfeldsgade 52**
**Copenhagen N** ④
*www.olsnedkeren.dk*

Since 2012, the team behind the microbrewery Ølsnedkeren (the name means 'the beer carpenter') have been growing a strong local following. Tip: enjoy large beers for the price of small beers during Monday happy hour.

102 MIKKELLER BAR

# *The 5 best bars for*
# JAZZ & BLUES

---

**106 JAZZHUS MONTMARTRE**
Store Regnegade 19A
Copenhagen K ①
+45 3172 3494
*www.jazzhus*
*montmartre.dk*

Since the late 1950s, Jazzhus Montmartre has been the epicenter for jazz in Copenhagen. During the 1960s, the club was frequented by the likes of Dexter Gordon, Ben Webster, Stan Getz, Kenny Drew, and many others. Today, the historic club still operates as a musical venue in the evenings and a cafe and bar during the daytime.

**107 BEVAR'S**
Ravnsborggade 10B
Copenhagen N ④
+45 5059 0993
*www.bevars.dk*

Bevar's is a stylish but low-key neighbourhood cafe that openly welcomes people to come in and work, have meetings, and study. Several nights a week, this creative cafe transforms into a venue where drinkers can enjoy live jazz music for free.

## 108 KIND OF BLUE

**Ravnsborggade 17**
**Copenhagen N** ④
**+45 2635 1056**
*www.kindofblue.dke*

Despite being named for Miles Davis' classic album, this isn't a 'jazz only' bar. But jazz lovers should make their way to Ravnsborggade anyway, because this cosy cafe often features live jazz in the evenings and always features good vibes, local characters, and great beer.

## 109 PALÆ BAR

**Ny Adelgade 5**
**Copenhagen K** ①
**+45 3312 5471**
*www.palaebar.dk*

It's true that this upscale bodega is primarily populated with a local, older crowd meeting up to talk politics, play chess, or argue about jazz, but Palæ Bar is also the official venue for Copenhagen's annual summer Jazz Festival. Palæ Bar has live jazz performances throughout the year.

## 110 MOJO BLUES BAR

**Løngangstræde 21C**
**Copenhagen K** ①
**+45 3311 6453**
*www.mojo.dk*

With live blues, jazz, rock, zydeco, and bluegrass music on the menu almost every night, this rugged old-school blues bar is one of the most dependable places in town to hear live music. But don't expect anything too fancy at Mojo – just a smoky atmosphere, a few classic drinks, and soulful music.

# *The 5 hippest*
# COCKTAIL BARS

---

### 111 LIDKOEB

**Vesterbrogade 72B**
**Copenhagen V** ③
*www.lidkoeb.dk*

Located in an historic building hidden just off of busy Vesterbrogade, Lidkoeb is three storeys of romantic ambiance, impeccable Danish design, and amazing mixed drinks (they also serve artisanal beers). Tip: Make sure to visit the gorgeous whisky bar on the top floor.

### 112 RUBY

**Nybrogade 10**
**Copenhagen K** ①
**+45 3393 1203**
*www.rby.dk*

There is no name on the door, no sign pointing the way; you just have to search for Ruby until you find it. But once you do, you will enter into Copenhagen's most legendary spot for cocktails. Since 2007, Ruby has been charming patrons with its low-lit interiors, friendly vibe, and extraordinary seasonal cocktails.

### 113 THE UNION BAR

**Store Strandstræde 19**
**Copenhagen K** ①

After entering this elusive 'speakeasy' via an unmarked door, a secret doorbell, and stairs down into the cellar, guests are invited to step back in time and embrace The Union's prohibition-era vibe, complete with vintage music, dim lights, and leather-aproned bar staff.

114 **DUCK AND COVER**
**Dannebrogsgade 6**
**Copenhagen V** ③
**+45 2812 4290**
*www.duckandcoverbar.dk*

Beneath the cool, distinctly mid-century modern interiors – think Scandinavian Mad Men, Duck and Cover – is essentially a really friendly neighbourhood cocktail bar. The space is intimate, the staff are enthusiastic, and the music is always perfectly in line with the bar's unpretentious vibe.

115 **CURFEW**
**Stenosgade 1**
**Copenhagen V** ③
**+45 2929 9276**
*www.curfew.dk*

Occupying a site that has played host to all kinds of bars since the early 20th century, this place has seen its fair share of heroes and villains – ask about the bullet holes in the walls. Recommended: the 'Unfaithful', made with Hendricks gin, cucumber, lemon juice, Cointreau, raw licorice, and honey.

112 RUBY

## The 5 best places to
# DRINK LIKE A LOCAL

---

116 **MC.KLUUD**
Istedgade 126
Copenhagen V ③
+45 3331 6383
*www.mckluud.dk*

In Copenhagen, a bodega is distinct from other kinds of bars for a few reasons: one, bodegas serve primarily – or exclusively – beer, two, you can smoke in most bodegas and, three, bodegas are typically filled with locals. The Western-themed Mc.Kluud on Istedgade is a classic example of the Danish bodega, serving up cheap drinks, jukebox tunes, and friendly, vintage vibes.

117 **VINSTUE 90**
Gammel Kongevej 90
Frederiksberg ⑥
+45 3331 8490
*www.vinstue90.dk*

Since 1916, the atmosphere at this beer bar has been simple and unpretentious, but what makes Vinstue 90 so special is the house's uncarbonated 'slow beer'. The slow version of Carlsberg served here is a smoother, creamier, froth-topped brew which takes around 15 minutes to pour.

### 118 DYREHAVEN

Sønder Boulevard 72
Copenhagen V ③
*www.dyrehavenkbh.dk*

Dyrehaven is a local bodega that has evolved into a more modern-style bar, serving quality meals all day, including traditional Danish smørrebrød, and catering to a younger, hipper crowd.

### 119 ALLÉENBERG

Allégade 4
Frederiksberg ⑥
+45 3325 4442
*www.alleenberg.dk*

Dark interiors, ancient furniture, and a steady stream of regulars give this venerable parkside pub (established in 1924) a very particular and comfortable atmosphere. Tip: ask the bar staff about the bar's nickname, 'the psychopath'.

### 120 ROSENGÅRDENS BODEGA

Rosengården 11
Copenhagen K ①
+45 3312 4625

A central Copenhagen pub known for its dark interiors, stained glass windows, simple food, and its handful of sidewalk tables and chairs. Cosier than most, Rosengårdens is a classier kind of bodega and also serves wine alongside its extensive beer list.

118 DYREHAVEN

# *The 5 most impressive*
# BEER LISTS

---

### 121 CAFE BANG & JENSEN

**Istedgade 130**
**Copenhagen V** ③
**+45 3325 5318**
*www.bangogjensen.dk*

This quirky bar is a favourite haunt among Vesterbro's hipsters, students, and beer aficionados alike. Housed in an old pharmacy, Cafe Bang & Jensen is styled with a mid-modern aesthetic and serves simple but quality food – especially their weekend brunch – and a long list of excellent beers on tap and in bottle, all at fair prices.

### 122 ØRSTED ØLBAR

**Nørre Farimagsgade 13**
**Copenhagen K** ①
**+45 3393 6575**
*www.oerstedoelbar.dk*

With over 100 bottled beers and another 20 craft brews on tap, including Mikkeller, the newly renovated Ørsted Ølbar offers a vast wealth of beers to enjoy. Located across the street from the charming Ørsted Park, Ørsted Ølbar is a local favourite situated well off the typical tourist path.

### 123 JERNBANECAFEEN

**Reventlowsgade 16**
**Copenhagen V** ③
**+45 3321 6090**
*www.jernbanecafeen.dk*

Just west of Copenhagen's central train station is the lively Jernbanecafeen, also known as 'the railroad pub', which has been in operation since 1933. This bodega stays open late every night and is home to a long list of Danish beers on tap, including a series of custom house beers brewed by Thisted Bryghus.

### 124 SØERNES ØLBAR

**Sortedam Dossering 83**
**Copenhagen Ø** ⑤
**+45 3219 6380**
*www.soernesoelbar.dk*

The lakeside sister of Ørsted Ølbar, Søernes Ølbar is one of the best beer bars in town. With a very impressive (and ever-evolving) menu of drafts and bottled beers, Søernes Ølbar is the perfect spot for enjoying a few drinks by the Copenhagen lakes. They also show lots of live sporting events, just in case you want to watch the game.

### 125 BERLIN BAR

**Gammel Kongevej 147**
**Frederiksberg** ⑥
**+45 3252 0171**
*www.berlin-bar.dk*

Berlin Bar is the only German beer bar in Copenhagen. With over 100 bottle varieties and another 15 beers on tap, Berlin Bar is a cosy neighbourhood bar that prides itself on sharing live football, good music, and the best German brews with the city's beer enthusiasts.

# *The 5 most stylish*
# HOTEL BARS

126 **SKOVSHOVED BAR**
SKOVESHOVED HOTEL
**Strandvejen 267**
**Charlottenlund** ⑧
**+45 3964 0028**
*www.skovshovedhotel.dk*

Everything about this historic, seaside hotel is romantic. And, luckily, you don't have to spend several hundreds of euros a night in order to experience the charms of this hidden gem. Instead, a visit to the hotel's friendly wine bar offers a chance to soak up the ambiance on the hotel's sunny terrace or its fireside lounge.

127 **NIMB BAR**
NIMB HOTEL
**Bernstorffsgade 5**
**Copenhagen K** ①
**+45 8870 0000**
*www.nimb.dk*

The award-winning Nimb Hotel is all about sophistication and luxury. The Nimb Bar, occupying the hotel's original ballroom, is a no-less elegant affair. With its open fireplace, crystal chandeliers, and ornate floral arrangements, this is a special occasion bar with an exclusive atmosphere.

128 **BALTHAZAR**
HOTEL D'ANGLETERRE
**Ny Østergade 6**
**Copenhagen K** ①
**+45 3312 1262**
*www.balthazarcph.dk*

Located at Kongens Nytorv, the elegant Hotel d'Angleterre is *la grande dame* of Copenhagen's many posh hotels. The exclusive Balthazar at Hotel d'Angleterre was the city's first champagne bar and offers several dozens of varieties of bubbly to choose from.

## 129 THE LIBRARY BAR

COPENHAGEN PLAZA HOTEL
**Bernstorffsgade 4**
**Copenhagen K** ①
**+45 3314 9262**
*www.librarybar.dk*

Dark wood panelling, leather bound books, classical paintings, and chesterfield sofas help to make The Library Bar one of the most timeless establishments in Copenhagen. The Library Bar is also well-known as a great place to relax and enjoy jazz.

## 130 BAR ROUGE

SKT. PETRI HOTEL
**Krystalgade 22**
**Copenhagen K** ①
**+45 3345 9100**
*www.sktpetri.com*

Located in the heart of the Latin Quarter, Bar Rouge at the designer Sankt Petri Hotel is an upscale, modernist bar with a reputation for excellent cocktails and an international crowd. Catering to business travellers, this bar is open late every night, and offers a wide selection of drinks with a relaxed lounge vibe.

126 SKOVSHOVED HOTEL

# The 5 best
# WINE BARS

---

**131 MALBECK**
Istedgade 61
Copenhagen V ③
+45 3331 1970
*www.malbeck.dk*

Vesterbro's Malbeck wine bar specializes in Argentinean wines, old school music, and intimate neighbourhood vibes. Tip: the first Friday of each month, Malbeck offers a wine tasting (six to eight wines) for only 150 kroner.

**132 BEAU MARCHÉ**
Ny Østergade 32
Copenhagen K ①
+45 5577 1430
*www.beaumarche.dk*

Tucked away in a quiet courtyard, this wine bar feels like a lovely corner of Paris has been transplanted into Copenhagen's city centre. Along with an outstanding list of wines, most available by the glass, Beau Marché offers French meals, coffee, and a perfect escape from the city outside.

**133 VILLA VINO**
Mikkel Bryggers Gade 11
Copenhagen K ①
+45 3332 1733
*www.villavino.dk*

Located across the street from the elegant Grand Theatre, this bustling, traditional wine bar has the energy of a busy Parisian cafe and an extensive, reasonably-priced wine menu. Tucked away just off of the Strøget, Villa Vino is a low-key bar and a favourite for the pre- and post-cinema crowd.

## 134 **VINBODEGAEN**
**Smallegade 39**
**Frederiksberg** ⑥
**+45 7070 7598**
*www.vinbodegaen.dk*

One of the city's newest wine bars, the cosy Vinbodegaen is a part of the family of wine-centric bars and restaurants owned by Danish wine guru Kenn Husted. Over 40 wines are available by the glass. Recommended: order a tin of fish and/or a plate of charcuterie with your *vino*.

## 135 **MAVEN**
**Nikolaj Plads 10-12**
**Copenhagen K** ①
**+45 3220 1100**
*www.restaurantmaven.dk*

Maven Restaurant and Wine Bar is located in the city's historic, repurposed Nikolaj Church, and the atmosphere here is highly romantic. Whether you come for the Nordic cuisine or to enjoy samplings from the extensive wine cellar, Maven is an unforgettable Copenhagen experience.

# The 5 best places to
# B Y O B
## (bring your own beer)

---

### 136 SØNDER BOULEVARD
**Copenhagen V** ③

Copenhagen has very generous laws when it comes to drinking alcohol in public. Especially in the summer months, when any spot in town can be transformed into an outdoor bar. One of the most popular of these spontaneous drinking spots is the tree-lined middle portion of Sønder Boulevard, which was converted into a belt of green spaces in 2007.

### 137 DRONNING LOUISES BRO
**Copenhagen N** ④

This bridge links Copenhagen's city centre and the diverse, artistic Nørrebro district. In recent years it has become the spot for the area's students, couples, and hipsters to sit in the sun and enjoy a six-pack of Danish brew.

### 138 ØSTRE ANLÆG PARK
**Stockholmsgade 20**
**Copenhagen Ø** ⑤

This park is a beloved local hangout of winding paths, rolling lawns, and scenic urban lakes. And in fine weather, this idyllic space is perfect for a long picnic brunch in the sun or an after-work 'happy hour' in the shade.

**139 SVANEMØLLEN BEACH**
Strandpromenaden 27
Copenhagen Ø ⑤

This new urban beach is located at the northeastern edge of Østerbro with views toward the evolving Nordhavn district and Sweden beyond. When the sun is out, this patch of sand and pier is packed with sunbathers, swimmers, and barbecuing Copenhageners.

**140 THE HARBOUR STEPS AT SØREN KIERKEGAARD PLADS**
Copenhagen K ①

The harbourfront steps located at Søren Kierkegaard Plads are one of the best fair-weather gathering places in central Copenhagen. Nestled between the iconic Royal Library and the bubble-like 'Dome of Visions', this is a cosy public terrace just waiting for visitors.

137 DRONNING LOUISES BRO

## *The 5 best*
# COFFEE BARS
## *in central Copenhagen*

---

### 141 DEMOCRATIC COFFEE BAR
**Krystalgade 15**
**Copenhagen K** ⓘ
**+45 4019 6237**

Attached to Copenhagen's bustling central library, Democratic Coffee Bar has become an essential destination for local and visiting coffee aficionados. Along with serving locally roasted, single-origin coffee, Democratic can also boast being the official home to 'Copenhagen's best croissant'.

### 142 COPENHAGEN COFFEE LAB
**Boldhusgade 6**
**Copenhagen K** ⓘ
**+45 4294 0419**
*www.cphcoffeelab.com*

Located in a cosy cellar just beneath the cobblestones of Boldhusgade is the minimalist coffee oasis of Copenhagen Coffee Lab. The CCL keeps it simple – no bells and whistles – just micro-roasted coffee served with passion.

### 143 CLARRODS INTERIOR
**Store Strandstræde 19**
**Copenhagen K** ⓘ
**+45 7199 1109**
*www.clarrods.com*

Just around the corner from tourist-soaked Nyhavn, is the stylish Clarrods cafe and design showroom. Besides serving excellent coffee and food, Clarrods is one of the few places in town where you can actually buy the Danish designed, raw urban furniture used in the cafe.

## 144 FORLOREN ESPRESSO

**Store Kongensgade 32**
**Copenhagen K** ①
*www.forlorenespresso.dk*

Every drink served in this tiny coffee bar is an expression of owner Niels H.S. Nielsen's passion for the intimate details of making great coffee. Coffee enthusiasts will appreciate Nielsen's stated distinction that his shop on Store Kongensgade is a coffee bar, 'not a cafe'.

## 145 ORIGINAL COFFEE AT ILLUM

**Østergade 52**
**Copenhagen K** ①
**+45 3318 2793**

Original Coffee is the newest – and best – of the coffee chains popping up around Copenhagen. But what makes this specific Original Coffee so special is its location on the top floor of the impressive Illum department store. Come for the coffee, stay for the epic views looking out over the city.

141 DEMOCRATIC COFFEE BAR

## *The 5 best*
# NEIGHBOURHOOD COFFEE BARS

---

146 **LA ESQUINA**
Ryesgade 7
Copenhagen Ø ⑤
+45 3536 3336
*www.laesquina.dk*

La Esquina is located pretty far off the typical tourist path, but for the people living and working around Ryesgade, this place is an oasis for those in need of a proper cup of coffee, a healthy lunch, or a glass or two of Spanish wine.

147 **KENT'S KAFFE LABORATORIUM**
Nørre Farimagsgade 70
Copenhagen K ①
+45 3311 1315
*www.kentkaffe laboratorium.com*

Part coffee bar, part science lab, Kent's KAFFE Lab is a coffee bar unlike any other in Copenhagen. The team at Kent's take coffee very seriously and love to talk about the how, why, and where of their beans, processes, and equipment.

148 **CENTRAL CAFÉ**
Tullinsgade 1
Copenhagen V ③
+45 2615 0186
*www.centralhotelogcafe.dk*

Located underneath the so-called 'smallest hotel in the world', the Central Café on Tullinsgade is a beloved neighbourhood haunt, rich in history and local pride. Tip: with only five seats inside the cafe, it's best to sit outside, where there's plenty of room to take in the ambiance of the charming street.

## 149 THE COFFEE COLLECTIVE

**Jægersborggade 10**
**Copenhagen N** ④
**+45 6015 1525**
*www.coffeecollective.dk*

By now you've likely heard of The Coffee Collective, who opened Copenhagen's first open coffee roastery in 2008. And while any one of the brand's award-winning, sustainably-focused locations will serve you a perfect coffee, the original on Jægersborggade still has that lovely neighbourhood vibe.

## 150 PROPS COFFEE SHOP

**Blågårdsgade 5**
**Copenhagen N** ④
**+45 3536 9955**
*www.propscoffeeshop.dk*

When it comes to finding an authentic neighbourhood coffee bar, look no further than Props Coffee Shop. Located on the walking street of Blågårdsgade and tucked in between galleries, secondhand shops, and dive bars, this place is always full of local characters and lively conversation.

149 THE COFFEE COLLECTIVE

## *The 5 cosiest*

# CAFES FOR
# A RAINY DAY

---

### 151 BASTARD CAFÉ

**Rådhusstræde 13**
**Copenhagen K** ①
**+45 4274 6642**
*www.bastardcafe.dk*

A cafe for board games, card games, coffee and *hygge*, Bastard Café is a unique place to skipp a few hours of bad weather by getting cosy with a favourite non-digital game. Many games are free to play, some require a small fee to 'rent,' and non-gamers are always welcome to come and learn.

### 152 IPSEN & CO

**Gammel Kongevej 108**
**Frederiksberg** ⑥
**+45 3214 5527**
*www.ipsenogco.dk*

If you're ever in Frederiksberg, whether in rain or sunshine, a visit to Ipsen & Co is always a good idea. Though primarily a coffee bar, Ipsen & Co is renowned for their brunch, baked goods, and their cosy, rustic interiors. Recommended: the house's homemade mulled wine.

### 153 CAFE RETRO

**Knabrostræde 26**
**Copenhagen K** ①
*www.cafe-retro.dk*

This cosy, volunteer-run cafe is one of the most atmospheric in central Copenhagen. With its comfy sofas, hidden alcoves, and ancient wooden beams, Café Retro is the perfect hide-out from the rain or snow. Note: all of Café Retro's profits go to support good causes in India and Africa.

## 154 VOULEZ-VOUS

**Larsbjørnsstræde 20**
**Copenhagen K** ①
**+45 9197 5719**
*www.voulezvous.dk*

This authentic French cafe and bistro is split into two levels, the dimly-lit cellar and the first floor with views overlooking the street. Both levels are perfect for taking a coffee break or escaping a rainy Danish day. Highly recommended is the house's homemade ginger and mint tea.

## 155 PARTERRE

**Overgaden Oven**
**Vandet 90**
**Christianshavn** ②

Opened by a father-son team in 2014, Parterre has quickly become a favourite destination for Copenhagen cafe enthusiasts – and Instagrammers. With a menu of simple food and outstanding coffee from the Swedish roastery Koppi, the genuinely friendly vibe at Parterre invites guests to come in and stay a while.

155 PARTERRE

# *The 5 best*
# SPECIALTY DRINKS
# SHOPS

———

156 **VINHANEN**
    **Baggesensgade 13**
    **Copenhagen N** ④
    *www.vinhanen.dk*

Instead of selling individual bottles of imported wine, Vinhanen imports giant vats of wine from Italy and France and then do the bottling themselves – one at a time – thus keeping prices low. After tasting a few glasses at the bar, you can take home your favourite bottle(s).

157 **DEN SIDSTE DRÅBE**
    **Jægersborggade 6**
    **Copenhagen N** ④
    **+45 2982 9637**

Den Sidste Dråbe (the last drop) co-owners Naja and Frederik run one of Copenhagen's most niche drinks shops. Specializing in 'white' liquors such as vodka and gin, this is a great place to discover your new favourite bottle of spirits.

158 **ØLBUTIKKEN**
    **Istedgade 44**
    **Copenhagen V** ③
    **+45 3322 0304**

Beloved by locals and sought out by beer geeks from around the world, Ølbutikken offers an almost overwhelming selection of Danish microbrews and unique beers from Europe and the US. The staff here really know their stuff and are happy to answer questions and offer advice. Recommended: try the house beer, 'Istedgade Hipster Ale'.

159 **JUUL'S WINE & SPIRITS**
Værnedamsvej 15
Frederiksberg ⑥
+45 3331 1329
*www.juuls.dk*

This classic shop has it all: wines, spirits, whiskies, organic spirits, champagne, and a lot of years of expertise. Nestled in among specialty boutiques and cateries, Juul's brings a long tradition of knowledge to this small hipster street.

160 **MIKKELLER BOTTLE SHOP**
Stefansgade 35
Copenhagen N ④
+45 3583 1020
*www.mikkeller.dk*

Fans of Copenhagen's iconic Mikkeller Bar will be thrilled to explore Mikkeller Bottle Shop located just four kilometres away in Nørrebro. The Bottle Shop carries around 200 different beers, including varieties from Mikkeller (Denmark), Three Floyds (USA), and numerous 'other praiseworthy microbreweries from around the world' that Mikkeller considers friends.

160 MIKKELLER BOTTLE SHOP

OLD

# 85 PLACES TO SHOP

# The 5 best shops for
# MEN'S FASHION

—————

### 161 GOODS

Østerbrogade 44
Copenhagen Ø ⑤
+45 3543 0505
*www.shop.goodscph.com*

By curating an ever-evolving collection that features both classic American brands, such as Red Wing and Levi's, as well as up-and-coming Danish designers, such as Norse Projects and Capital Goods, GOODS owner Kasper Hostrup has crafted one of the most stylish menswear shops in the city.

### 162 HAN KJØBENHAVN

Vognmagergade 7
Copenhagen K ①
*www.hankjobenhavn.com*

Originally, Han Kjøbenhavn was in the eyewear business, but since 2008 the brand has expanded into one of Scandinavia's premier fashion brands. Also, their flagship store on Vognmagergade is a mid-century architectural gem that shows off the current Han Kjøbenhavn collection in impeccable style.

### 163 MARITIME ANTIQUES

Toldbodgade 15
Copenhagen K ①
+45 3312 1257
*www.maritime-antiques.dk*

This curious antiques-cum-menswear boutique is unlike any other shop in Copenhagen. Located in a basement space on historic Toldbodgade, owners Frans and Magali have curated a fascinating collection of gorgeous nautical antiques for sale alongside specialty Scandinavian fashion brands such as S.N.S Herning, HANSEN, and Andersen-Andersen.

### 164 NO NATIONALITY 07

Gammel Mønt 7
Copenhagen K ⓘ
+45 3841 1141
www.nn07.com

By bringing together Japanese aesthetics and Scandinavian simplicity, the Danish founders of No Nationality 07 (or NN07) have endeavored to 'go beyond monotone fashion'. The brand's concept store in central Copenhagen is the best place to get familiar with NN07's durable, adventure-inspired collections of modern menswear.

### 165 WARDROBE 19

Larsbjørnsstræde 19
Copenhagen K ⓘ
+45 3214 1312
www.wardrobe19.com

Wardrobe 19 is all about menswear essentials: leather boots, durable bags, and a carefully selected, seasonal collection of clothes and accessories. With rustic interiors, an expert staff, and a prime location on cosy Larsbjørnsstræde, Wardrobe 19 is a must-visit shop for admirers of the timeless traditions of manly style.

161 GOODS

# The 5 biggest shops for
# DANISH DESIGN

### 166 ILLUMS BOLIGHUS

Amagertorv 10
Copenhagen K ①
+45 3314 1941
*www.illumsbolighus.dk*

Illums Bolighus is a massive, multi-level department store dedicated exclusively to the very best of Danish and Scandinavian design. This 'temple to modern design' is overwhelming in all the best ways.

### 167 NORMANN COPENHAGEN

Østerbrogade 70
Copenhagen Ø ⑤
+45 3527 0540
*www.normann-copenhagen.com*

Recognised by *The New York Times* as one of the '12 Shopping Treasures of Europe', this concept store carries the full line of Normann Copenhagen's own design products as well as hundreds of other books, clothing, and interior products from fellow Scandinavian brands.

### 168 HAY HOUSE

Østergade 61
Copenhagen K ①
+45 42 820 820
*www.hay.dk*

In recent years, there has been no bigger name in Danish design than HAY. Inside the HAY House, the brand showcases their goods in the unique context of an apartment space overlooking Copenhagen's Amagertorv (Amager Square).

169 **PAUSTIAN**
Kalkbrænderiløbskaj 2
Copenhagen Ø ⑤
+45 3916 6565
www.paustian.dk

Located in a showroom designed by Danish architect Jørn Utzon (designer of the Sydney Opera House), Paustian has been a leading name in Danish design for decades. The shop showcases a sophisticated and elegant mixture of new design and classic Danish masterpieces.

170 **BOLIA**
Christian IX Gade 7
Copenhagen K ①
+45 3036 8948
www.bolia.com

Bolia is a rising star in the world of Danish design. Balancing practical Nordic minimalism with playful geometries, Bolia creates ingenious and (relatively) affordable furniture, lighting, housewares, and textiles.

168 **HAY HOUSE**

# The 5 best
# BOUTIQUE DESIGN
## shops

―――――――

### 171 MUNK

Torvegade 25
Christianshavn ②
+45 3336 5554
*www.munkshop.dk*

This award-winning boutique is the passion project of owner Hans Peter Munk, a longtime veteran of the Scandinavian design industry. With its stunning aesthetics and perfectly curated selection of brands, Munk has established itself as Christianshavn's best design shop.

### 172 DESIGNER ZOO

Vesterbrogade 137
Copenhagen V ③
+45 3324 9493
*www.dzoo.dk*

Part retail shop, part designer workshop, Designer Zoo is unlike any other design shop in Copenhagen. Since 1999, Designer Zoo has served two functions – one, sell great Danish design products, and two, invite local makers to collaborate and create on-site.

### 173 NOTRE DAME

Nørregade 7
Copenhagen K ①
+45 3315 1615
*www.notredame.dk*

This colourful shop carries a vast selection of Danish designed kitchenwares, linens, paper goods, lighting and small furniture. Every possible surface and wall of Notre Dame is covered in things you will want to take home for yourself or as a gift.

### 174 DANSKMADEFORROOMS

Istedgade 80
Copenhagen V ③
+45 3218 0255
*www.danskmade*
*forrooms.dk*

Opened by fashion designers (and sisters) Ma-lou and Malene Sofie Westendahl, DANSKmadeforrooms is a bespoke, influential leader among the city's many design shops. Every textile, lamp, poster, and chair featured at DANSK has been hand-selected for its timeless, enduring quality.

### 175 DESIGNDELICATESSEN

Frederiksberg Allé 6
Frederiksberg ⑥
+45 3311 1470
*www.designdelicatessen.dk*

The inspiring Designdelicatessen show-room on Frederiksberg Allé is a treasure trove of Scandinavian furniture, lamps, graphics and textiles. But the shop's lovely selection of products is only a sampling of Designdelicatessen's even larger online inventory of approximately 4000 items.

171 MUNK

## The 5 hippest
# SHOPPING STREETS
## to explore

---

**176 PILESTRÆDE**
City Centre
Copenhagen K ①

Parallel to the much busier shopping street Købmagergade, Pilestræde is dotted with fashionable shops, cosy cafes and funky bars. You will find everything from Scandinavian design for the home at HAY, to trendy streetwear sneakers at Naked.

**177 ISTEDGADE**
Vesterbro
Copenhagen V ③

Previously known as the heart of Copenhagen's Red Light District, Istedgade has gone through something of a renaissance. These days, the street is defined by a quirky mix of boutique shops, hipster bars, and a few remnants of its neon-coloured past. Recommended: Malbeck wine bar, DANSKmadeforrooms for design, and Rude for women's fashion.

**178 VÆRNEDAMSVEJ**
Vesterbro
Copenhagen V ③

Often compared to the lively streets of Paris, Værnedamsvej is home to some of Copenhagen's best specialty shops and eateries. Recommended: Dora for interior design, Les Trois Cochons for French cuisine, and Granola for coffee and lunch.

## 179 ELMEGADE

Nørrebro
Copenhagen N ④

Elmegade is a small side street that connects busy Nørrebrogade with Sankt Hans Torve, one of the district's most popular gathering places. Recommended: Acne Archive for Danish fashion, Hooha for sneakers, Velour for fashion, Laundromat Cafe for lunch, and Clarkes for coffee.

## 180 BLÅGÅRDSGADE

Nørrebro
Copenhagen N ④

Just a short walk from Elmegade, Blågårdsgade is mostly a car-free street, which makes it perfect for hanging out, shopping, and people watching. Recommended: Vaerkstedet for Danish design, Studio Travel for vintage fashion, Harbo Bar for beer, Beyti for shawarma, and Cafe Arabica for coffee.

178 **VÆRNEDAMSVEJ**

## The 5 best shops for
# MODERN STREETWEAR

---

**181 NORSE PROJECTS**
Pilestræde 41
Copenhagen K ⓘ
+45 3393 2626
*www.norsestore.com*

With its motto, 'created for life – good for all seasons', Norse Projects is the quintessentially sophisticated urban streetwear shop. Carrying top brands as well as its own label of men's and women's wear, the Norse Store is the epicenter of Copenhagen cool.

**182 LE FIX**
Kronprinsensgade 9B
Copenhagen K ⓘ
+45 8861 4101
*www.le-fix.com*

Founded by a group of childhood friends, united in their love of graffiti and hip-hop culture, Le Fix is more than a shop: the brand is a self-described 'constellation' made up of a clothing brand, a tattoo parlour, an art studio, and a woodshop.

**183 WOOD WOOD MUSEUM**
Frederiksborggade 54
Copenhagen K ⓘ
+45 3535 6264
*www.woodwood.dk*

Copenhagen's Wood Wood brand mixes high fashion, sports and streetwear with youth culture, art and music. The brand's high-end flagship store is located at Grønnegade 1, but the 'outlet style' Wood Wood Museum store is the better place to bargain hunt and find unique pieces.

### 184 SOULLAND

Gammel Kongevej 37
Copenhagen V ③
+45 5364 0186
www.soulland.com

Every year Soulland's two seasonal menswear collections inevitably garner accolades from the likes of *GQ, Euroman, ID Magazine* and others tastemakers. At their flagship store, Soulland's own wares are featured alongside other carefully curated and complimentary labels.

### 185 STREETMACHINE

Kronprinsensgade 3
Copenhagen K ①
+45 3333 9511
www.streetmachine.com

With origins in the gritty 1980s skateboarding scenes of Paris and California, Copenhagen's Streetmachine has been a source for trendsetting urban streetwear since the mid 1990s. While still focussed on Denmark's skate culture, today the curated brands of Streetmachine have an appeal that reaches far beyond the skatepark.

185 STREETMACHINE

# *The 5 best*
# BOOKSHOPS

---

**186 BOOKS & COMPANY**
Sofievej 1
Hellerup ⑧
+45 3930 4045
*www.booksandcompany.dk*

Over the last decade, Books & Company has become a beloved institution in the largely international community of northern Copenhagen. This quaint 'shop around the corner' specializes in English language books, magazines, newspapers, kids books, and an excellent coffee bar.

**187 ARK BOOKS**
Møllegade 10
Copenhagen N ④
+45 8165 5458
*www.arkbooks.dk*

The mission of this unique, non-profit shop is to introduce Danes to lesser known literature from around the world and to introduce the city's non-Danes to the best of Danish literature. This cosy shop is a great place to escape a rainy day. Step in, talk literature and drink a cup of free coffee.

**188 CINNOBER**
Landemærket 9
Copenhagen K ①
+45 2613 9833
*www.cinnobershop.dk*

This independent bookshop is run by Ulla Welinder and Morten Voigt, a graphic designer and illustrator duo, so you know the handpicked books, magazines, stationery, and designer goods at Cinnober are always going to be beautifully curated. This bespoke bookery is tucked away just off the main shopping street.

189 **THIEMERS MAGASIN**
Tullinsgade 24
Copenhagen V ③
+45 5059 5100
www.thiemers.dk

With a mix of English and Danish language books and magazines, Thiemers is the essence of what an independent bookshop should be: friendly, centrally located, with just the right mix of the new, the familiar, and the unexpected.

190 **POLITIKENS BOGHANDEL**
Rådhuspladsen 37
Copenhagen K ①
+45 3067 2806
www.politikensforlag.dk

Located in the very centre of the city, Politikens Boghandel is Copenhagen's biggest Danish and English language bookseller. With its extensive stock and friendly staff, there is a very good chance you will find the book you're looking for here.

186 **BOOKS & COMPANY**

# *The 5 best places for*
# GRAPHIC ART
# *and* PAPER

---

**191  PLAYTYPE**

Værnedamsvej 6
Copenhagen V ③
+45 6040 6914
*www.playtype.com*

Originally established as an experimental celebration of typography itself, Playtype has moved quickly to the forefront of creative graphic design coming out of Scandinavia. The ever-innovating Playtype shop in Værnedamsvej is a must-see for graphic design junkies.

**192  CMYK KLD**

Jægersborggade 51 kld
Copenhagen N ④
+45 2383 8904
*www.butikcmyk.dk*

Located alongside some of the city's hippest boutiques and eateries, CMYK kld is a delightful little place with a great big personality. With a focus on illustration and hand-drawn works, the shop is home to a wide range of affordable prints by artists from Copenhagen and around Denmark.

**193  STILLEBEN**

Niels Hemmingsens
Gade 3
Copenhagen K ①
+45 3391 1131
*www.stilleben.dk*

Stilleben is much more than a poster shop, but designer prints are certainly one of their specialties. Ditte and Jelena, the shop's two owners, are internationally renowned for running one of Copenhagen's most consistently reliable and trendsetting design boutiques.

### 194 LIMITED WORKS

Blågårdsgade 17
Copenhagen N ④
+45 6168 9844
www.limitedworks.com

This lovely gallery at the centre of artistic Blågårdsgade originated as an online store but is now the brick and mortar home to a wide variety of quality works of original art and prints by both emerging and established artists.

### 195 PAPER COLLECTIVE

Kompagnistræde 29
Copenhagen K ①
www.paper-collective.com

The Paper Collective team brings together designers, illustrators, photographers and agencies from all around the world to create inspirational and iconic art prints in limited editions of less than 700 pieces and each collection is linked to a good cause somewhere in the world.

195 PAPER COLLECTIVE

## *The 5 best*
# RECORD SHOPS

196 **GOODLIFE**
Stefansgade 12
Copenhagen N ④
+45 2639 1985

This little corner shop does two of life's simple pleasures very well: coffee and music. Located on the corner of Søllerødgade and Stefansgade, GoodLife is a quiet neighbourhood hangout that specializes in indie rock, soul, and classic records.

197 **ÆTER RECORD STORE**
Jægersborggade 50
Copenhagen N ④
+45 6085 6564
*www.neh-owh.com*

Æter record store is Copenhagen's mecca for rare and experimental music. This shop is the go-to spot for unknown artists and unusual sounds. They have vintage videogames as well.

198 **SORT KAFFE & VINYL**
Skydebanegade 4
Copenhagen V ③
+45 6170 3349

The name of this cosy shop says it all: black coffee and vinyl. Serving up a diverse selection of quality records, from new releases to reissues to classic discs, as well as serving very good coffee, this hip Vesterbro shop is located just a block off of Istedgade, but is well worth a visit, especially when the sun is out and the terrace is open.

## 199 **ROUTE 66**

Fælledvej 3
Copenhagen N ④
+45 3535 6560

Route 66 offers up primarily new records from mainstream artists as well as indie bands. The shop's secondhand records are in the basement. One thing that sets Route 66 apart is its offering of vintage and contemporary Danish language records.

## 200 **SOUND STATION**

Gammel Kongevej 94
Frederiksberg ⑥
+45 3321 4043
www.soundstation.dk

First opened back in 1991, Frederiksberg's Sound Station prides itself on the quality and diversity of its vinyl stock. Home to a wide range of musical genres, Sound Station specializes in a wall-to-wall collection of everything from rockabilly to punk and from jazz to metal. With new stock arriving everyday, this place is a vinyl hunter's dream.

# *The 5 best custom*
# BIKE SHOPS

---

### 201 SÖGRENI

Sankt Peders
Stræde 30A
Copenhagen K ①
+45 3312 7879
*www.sogrenibikes.com*

A big part of what makes Sögreni so special is that, despite their streamlined design-build process, these guys don't do mass production; each and every bike is made as a partnership between the customer and the craftsmen.

### 202 LARRY VS. HARRY

Frederiksborggade 43
Copenhagen K ①
+45 3136 1719
*www.larryvsharry.com*

This shop has made a name for itself by producing the sleek and stylish Bullitt, a cargo-style bike designed to 'replace much of the functions of a car in the city, but that would also be a desirable object'. The Larry vs. Harry showroom on Frederiksborggade is a must-visit for gear heads and design junkies alike.

### 203 CYKELFABRIKKEN

Istedgade 92
Copenhagen V ③
+45 2712 3232
*www.cykelfabrikken.dk*

Christian and Oscar of Cykelfabrikken build amazing bicycles from quality materials and with a passion for their craft – simple as that. A visit to the ultra-cool Cykelfabrikken shop on Istedgade is a visit to a minimalist shrine to the glory cycle-building.

## 204 CYKELMAGEREN

Store Kongensgade 57
Copenhagen K ⓘ
+45 3311 1211
www.cykelmageren.dk

Since 1994, Rasmus Gjesing of Cykelmageren (the bike maker) has been making bikes that are works of art. With a remarkable attention to details, Rasmus' bikes are each made by hand, one at a time.

## 205 VELORBIS

Nørre Farimagsgade 63
Copenhagen K ⓘ
+45 3811 2277
www.velorbis.com

With a brand motto like 'Ride in Style', you better make stylish bicycles. But true to their word, Velorbis makes some of the coolest bikes now cruising the streets of Copenhagen. With an emphasis on classic design, cyclist posture, and timeless 'cycle chic', the Velorbis brand is gaining much-deserved respect worldwide.

201 SÖGRENI

## The 5 best local
# JEWELLERY DESIGNERS

---

### 206 MARIA BLACK

Silkegade 13
Copenhagen K ①
+45 3311 5066
www.maria-black.com

By using highly dramatic geometries, dark colours, and experimental, interchangeable design elements, Copenhagen designer Maria Black has been creating innovative jewellery collections since 2010.

### 207 MOSS COPENHAGEN

Kronprinsensgade 7
Copenhagen K ①
+45 4130 1101
www.mosscopenhagen.com

This Danish fashion brand has grown exponentially over the past few years, expanding to include menswear and a branded cafe in Nørrebro. But what Moss does best is their affordable line of minimalist designer jewellery.

### 208 LINE & JO

Gothersgade 31
Copenhagen K ①
+45 3514 1499
www.lineandjo.com

At the high end of the Danish jewellery scene is Line & Jo, whose self-described style is 'raw lady punk with feminine grace, simplistic minimalism with classic aesthetics'. But however you interpret their style, the jewellery of design duo Line Hallberg and Jo Riis-Hansen is a favourite among Copenhageners.

### 209 VIBE HARSLØF

*www.vibeharsloef.dk*
AT WOOD WOOD BOUTIQUE
Grønnegade 1
Copenhagen K ①
+45 3535 6264
*www.woodwood.dk*

With creations falling somewhere between playfully bohemian and starkly Scandinavian, jewellery designer Vibe Harsløf's work is influenced by the convergence of street culture and Denmark's rich design tradition. You can shop Vibe's work online, at boutiques around Copenhagen and at the Danish Design Museum.

### 210 KATRINE KRISTENSEN

*www.katrine kristensen.com*
AT KK BOUTIQUE
Gammel Kongevej 37
Copenhagen V ③
+45 6179 7709
AT HENRIK VIBSKOV BOUTIQUE
Krystalgade 6
Copenhagen K ①
+45 3314 6100

With collections named 'Talesman', 'Armour', 'Bubbles' and 'Bullets', the jewellery of designer Katrine Kristensen is certainly intriguing, both visually and conceptually. Another Copenhagen designer taking inspiration from counter-culture, Kristensen's jewellery challenges the status quo and makes a bold statement.

# The 5 best shops for
# HIS & HERS FASHION

**211 SAMSØE & SAMSØE**
Pilestræde 8C
Copenhagen K ⓘ
+45 3528 5111
*www.samsoe.com*

One of the most continually relevant and fashionable boutiques in Copenhagen, Samsøe is where modern streetwear meets Scandinavian chic. There are several Samsøe locations in town, but the shop on Pilestræde is the best – with an ever-changing selection of fresh and creative men's and women's fashion.

**212 MADS NØRGAARD**
Amagertorv 15
Copenhagen K ⓘ
+45 3332 0128
*www.madsnorgaard.dk*

Mads Nørgaard's modern interpretations of fashion classics have become iconic among Copenhagen's young, artistic crowd. Though never straying too far from time-tested prints, classic stripes, and Scandinavian knits, Nørgaard's thoughtful collections are always moving fashion forward.

### 213 STORM COPENHAGEN

Store Regnegade 1
Copenhagen K ①
+45 3393 0014
*www.stormfashion.dk*

Since 2001, Storm Copenhagen's concept store on Store Regnegade has been setting trends and challenging the idea of what a retail space can be. By incorporating books, art, skin care products, music, and magazines alongside high-end fashion brands, Storm has made a name for itself as Copenhagen's premier lifestyle shop.

### 214 KYOTO

Istedgade 95
Copenhagen V ③
+45 3331 6636
*www.kyoto.dk*

This trendy multi-brand shop has been around since 2001 and carries a variety of the best Scandinavian brands, such as Selected, Wood Wood, and Le Fix. In addition to selling great clothing, Kyoto's relaxed vibe and friendly staff are a welcome change from the hustle and bustle of the central shopping district.

### 215 SELECTED

Frederiksberg Centret
Falkoner Allé 21
Frederiksberg ⑥
+45 3888 9939
*www.selected.com*

The SELECTED brand has been growing steadily since 1997, when it was founded as a modern Nordic menswear label. Since then, SELECTED has expanded to include SELECTED Femme for women. With a focus on classic sophistication and subtle glamour, SELECTED is a sure bet for the essential fashion needs of today's urbanites.

## *The 5 coolest*
# VINTAGE CLOTHING
## *shops*

---

**216 STUDIO TRAVEL**
Blågårdsgade 14
Copenhagen N ④
+45 2684 1260

White interiors, vintage treasures for men and women, hip magazines, and a very cool shop owner make Studio Travel on Blågårdsgade a neighbourhood favourite for vintage clothing and for hanging out.

**217 KØBENHAVN K**
Studiestræde 32
Copenhagen K ①
+45 3373 1519

København K has two locations: the larger of their two vintage shops is on Studiestræde and the more boutique-esque shop is on nearby Teglgårdsstræde. The main store on Studiestræde is hidden off of the main street, so look for the 'K' sign hanging over the entry into the courtyard.

**218 O-S-V.**
Peder Hvitfeldts Stræde 4
Copenhagen K ①
+45 3210 4222
*www.o-s-v.dk*

In a city where fashion is never cheap, at least there is a shop like O-S-V. that both feels like a designer boutique and carries exciting Scandinavian brands for men and women (such as Stine Goya, Norse Projects, and Ganni) at below high street prices. New inventory arrives at O-S-V. every day.

### 219 TIME'S UP VINTAGE

Krystalgade 4
Copenhagen K ①
+45 3332 3930
www.timesupshop.com

It's no wonder that stylists and designers are often seen popping into Time's Up Vintage for professional inspiration and/or to top-up their own wardrobes. The emphasis is on vintage luxury brands and retro glamour pieces.

### 220 PRAG

Vesterbrogade 98A
Copenhagen V ③
+45 3379 0050

Nørrebrogade 45
Copenhagen N ④
+45 3321 0050
www.pragcopenhagen.com

Beloved by local enthusiasts as 'vintage heaven,' both of the impressive PRAG shops in Copenhagen are well-sourced, well-organised, and full of retro clothes from every era, even going back as far back as the 1920s. All of the inventory at PRAG is 'collected abroad and chosen based on current and future trends'. Unlike most shops in the capital, PRAG is open seven days a week.

# The 5 most inspiring
## Copenhagen based
# FASHION DESIGNERS

221 **HENRIK VIBSKOV**
HENRIK VIBSKOV BOUTIQUE
Krystalgade 6
Copenhagen K ①
+45 3314 6100
*www.henrikvibskov.com*

Vibskov's fashion creations are a marriage of funk and fantasy. And with every new season's collection, this rising Danish designer is garnering more and more international attention. The multi-brand Henrik Vibskov Boutique is a must visit for fashion lovers, who will revel in Vibskov's colourful, playful, and always surprising selection of clothing for men and women.

222 **ASTRID ANDERSEN**
AA BOUTIQUE
Jagtvej 19
Copenhagen N ④

Danish fashion designer Astrid Andersen is on a mission to 'fuse the worlds of luxury and sports'. Season after season, Andersen is pushing the boundaries of traditional menswear by intertwining tough-guy street style with contrastingly luxurious textures, colours, and silhouettes. Shop Astrid Andersen in Copenhagen at Storm on Store Regnegade or at the AA Boutique (only open on Saturdays).

## 223  CHARLOTTE ESKILDSEN
### FOR DESIGNERS REMIX

Charlotte Eskildsen is the creative director and founder of Danish fashion label Designers Remix. Ms. Eskildsen's seasonal collections draw inspiration from all areas of design, including Danish furniture classics, military designs, and the functionalist architecture of the 20th century.

## 224  RIKKE BAUMGARTEN AND HELLE HESTEHAVE
### FOR BAUM UND PFERDGARTEN

Vognmagergade 2
Copenhagen K ⓘ
+45 3530 1090
www.baumundpferd
garten.com

In 1999, designers Rikke Baumgarten and Helle Hestehave combined forces to create the very stylish brand Baum und Pferdgarten. By challenging the standard blacks of the 'Copenhagener's uniform', Baum und Pferdgarten bring a vibrant and playful dynamic to the Danish fashion scene.

## 225  LENE BORGGAARD
### FOR BRUUNS BAZAAR

Kronprinsensgade 8
Copenhagen K ⓘ
+45 3332 1999
www.bruunsbazaar.dk

Modern, elegant, minimalist – Lene Borggaard's creative work for Bruuns Bazaar is distinctly Scandinavian in its seemingly effortless simplicity. Winner of the 2013 ELLE Designer of the Year award, Ms. Borggaard's work is classic and accessible, ready for the real world, and not just the runway.

# The 5 best shops for
# WOMEN'S FASHION

---

### 226 STINE GOYA
Gothersgade 58
Copenhagen K ⓘ
+45 3217 1000
*www.stinegoya.com*

Since 2006, model-turned-designer Stine
Goya's shop has been a favourite among
Copenhagen's fashionistas. With her
playful designs, colourful prints, and
unique silhouettes, Ms. Goya's creations
are at once distinctly feminine and yet
unapologetically modern.

### 227 ANOTHER NUÉ
Krystalgade 3
Copenhagen K ⓘ
+45 3312 3302
*www.nuecph.coa*

Another nué is the larger, newer 'sister'
location to the original nué shop on
Gammel Kongevej in Frederiksberg. This
multi-brand, fashion-forward boutique
offers a hand-picked selection of clothing
and accessories from a wide range of
international designers, in both high-end
and casual wear.

### 228 DAY BIRGER ET MIKKELSEN
Pilestræde 16
Copenhagen K ⓘ
+45 3345 8880
*www.day.dk*

Producing seasonal lines that blend the
bohemian and the Scandinavian, DAY
Birger et Mikkelsen – and their more
youthful 2NDDAY brand – are essential
names in Danish women's wear.

## 229 **GANNI**

Store Regnegade 12
Copenhagen K ⓘ
+45 2088 5311
www.ganni.com

In 2014, Danish fashion darling Ganni was awarded 'Brand of the Year' by the Danish Elle Style Awards. The brand stands for a seemingly effortless 'Scandinavian chic' look. Mixing classic blacks with intriguing seasonal offerings, the flagship Ganni store at Store Regnegade never fails to impress.

## 230 **VILA**

Vimmelskaftet 43
Copenhagen K ⓘ
+45 3315 2244
www.vila.com

Combining trending looks with classic essentials, VILA is an international, Danish-based brand that has proven itself a dependable fashion source for the 'graceful and adventurous' modern woman. With multiple shops around the city, VILA offers Scandinavian style at the more affordable end of the price scale.

229 GANNI

# The 5 best
# VINTAGE FURNITURE
# AND DESIGN *shops*

---

231 **NO 40-COPENHAGEN**
Gammel Kongevej 39A
Copenhagen V ③
+45 3198 186
*www.no40.dk*

This stylish shop has a particularly cool and rugged character, with its collection of industrial equipment, steel lamps, old sports gear, vintage shelving, flags and richly textured antique wooden items.

232 **FINDERI**
Møntergade 14
Copenhagen K ①
+45 2622 1441
*www.finderi.dk*

Finderi is a quaint, centrally located boutique that specializes in vintage Scandinavian homewares such as ceramics, textiles, small furniture and wooden items, many of which are, most certainly, one-of-a-kind treasures.

233 **FIL DE FER**
Store Kongensgade 83
Copenhagen K ①
+45 3332 3246
*www.fildefer.dk*

Fil de Fer is one of Copenhagen's absolute finest curiosity shops. Packed from end to end with French antiques spanning a wide range of eras and places of origin, from elegant furniture to old Parisian lamps to retro medical supplies, this delightful place is part vintage shop, part 'museum of the bizarre'.

## 234 BIRKHOLM CPH

Vesterbrogade 79
Copenhagen V ③
+45 6146 4643
*www.birkholmcph.dk*

This cosy little shop is a two-for-one treat for design enthusiasts, with its carefully selected mixture of new Scandinavian design items alongside well-matched examples of retro furniture. Displayed here in complete design harmony, the elegant marriage of old and new at Birkholm CPH is truly inspiring.

## 235 OLD: VINTAGE FURNITURE & STUFF

Nørre Farimagsgade 53
Copenhagen K ①
+45 2117 3967
*www.oldkbh.dk*

Old is a wonderland of delightful vintage treasures, just waiting to be discovered, but with a more American sensibility. Colourful antique toys, musical instruments, and classic furniture and decor items anchor the personality of this friendly, neighbourhood shop. Note, Old is only open Thursday through Saturday afternoons.

235 OLD

# *The 5 most inspiring*
# DESIGN SHOWROOMS
## *to visit*

---

**236 FRAMA**

Frandericiagade 57
Copenhagen K ①
+45 3140 6030
www.framacph.com

The Frama showroom and offices are located in the historic St. Paul's pharmacy. This stunning interior space is a marriage of design traditions, combining 19th-century classicism with Frama's innovative lamps, furniture, and interior pieces. Call or email ahead to set up a visit.

**237 LOUIS POULSEN**

Gammel Strand 28
Copenhagen K ①
+45 7033 1414
www.louispoulsen.com

One of the very best places to experience the lamps of Denmark's most famous lighting designer, Poul Henningsen (known as PH), is at the inspiring Louis Poulsen showroom, which specializes in both classic and contemporary lamps from PH and other Danish designers.

**238 TOM ROSSAU**

Frederiksberg Allé 5
Copenhagen V ③
+45 5192 4707
www.tomrossau.dk

One of Denmark's most exciting contemporary lighting designers is Tom Rossau, whose workshop and flagship store are located in Frederiksberg. Known around the world for their distinct, sculptured forms, Rossau's elegant lamps are handcrafted from sculpted wood veneer and produced on site with impressive care and precision.

### 239 GUBI

Møntergade 19
Copenhagen K ①
+45 5361 6368
www.gubi.dk

Mixing the best of vintage forms with contemporary trends, Gubi's flagship space at Møntergade is home to the innovative, timeless design pieces that the brand believes will become the 'icons of the future'.

### 240 PAKHUS 48

Klubiensvej 22-24
Frihavn
Nordhavn ⑤
www.pakhus48.dk

Inside this 3000-square- metre converted warehouse are the six permanent design showrooms of GRID, Luceplan/ MODULAR, Erik Jørgensen, VOLA, Kvadrat and Montana, as well as rotating temporary exhibits and design pop-up shops from other brands.

236 FRAMA

# The 5
# DANISH DESIGNERS
## *you need to know*

241 **ARNE JACOBSEN (1902-1971)**

Architect, furniture maker, product designer, modernist thinker and creative genius Arne Jacobsen is a national hero in Denmark. With a résumé that includes commissions around the world, Jacobsen was the leader of the influential Danish Modern movement. Many of his works are now preserved as listed buildings and can be visited throughout Copenhagen.

242 **POUL HENNINGSEN (1894-1967)**

Known in Denmark simply as 'PH', Poul Henningsen is the most famous of the many famous Danish lamp and lighting designers. His elegant and geometric designs of the 1920s and 1930s were cutting-edge for the time period but are still widely popular around the world today.

### 243 **HANS WEGNER**
**(1914-2007)**

A contemporary and colleague of Arne Jacobsen, Wegner was a prolific chair designer, having designed over 500 original pieces of modern furniture during his career, many of which are still being produced today. Wegner once said: "The good chair is a task one is never completely done with."

### 244 **GEORG JENSEN**
**(1866-1935)**

From humble beginnings to international fame, Danish silversmith Georg Jensen is a hero of the Art Nouveau school of applied arts. His elegant yet functional cutlery, jewellery, vases, and decorative works have been admired, imitated, and reinterpreted for generations and continue to influence the work of artists of many disciplines.

### 245 **MARIE GUDME LETH**
**(1895-1997)**

Classically trained at the Copenhagen Royal Art Academy, artist and entrepreneur Marie Gudme Leth was a pioneer of Danish textile design in the first half of the 20th century. Her colourful, often whimsical, screen printed fabrics were introduced to the Danes in the 1930s and, remarkably, have never gone out of style.

12

TIETGEN STUDENT HALL

# 25 BUILDINGS
# TO ADMIRE

---

# The 5 finest
# CHURCHES
## in Copenhagen

---

**246 FREDERIK'S CHURCH**
Frederiksgade 4
Copenhagen K ①
+45 3315 0144
*www.marmorkirken.dk*

Just west of the royal residences of Amalienborg, the stately 'Marble Church' looks as if it has been imported to Denmark directly from Rome. Before being completed in 1894, this ornate church, with its massive dome, had a fascinating and troubled past, having been left as an unfinished ruin for almost 150 years. Today, this beloved church is open to the public.

**247 ST. ALBAN'S CHURCH**
Churchillparken 11
Copenhagen K ①
+45 3311 8518
*www.st-albans.dk*

Known by many as 'The English Church', St. Alban's is located on the eastern edge of the idyllic green Kastellet park and moat and just around the corner from *The Little Mermaid* statue. With its distinct Gothic Revival architecture and use of limestone and flint stones, St. Alban's is unique among churches in Copenhagen.

## 248 GRUNDTVIG'S CHURCH

På Bjerget 14B
Strandvejen ⑧
+45 3581 5442
*www.grundtvigskirke.dk*

Named for the Danish philosopher and hymn writer N.F.S. Grundtvig (1783-1872), this otherworldly church is unlike anything else you'll see in Copenhagen. Designed in the 1920s and built with over six million identical yellow bricks, Grundtvig's Church is a dramatic example of expressionist architecture that is definitely worth the short trip outside of the city centre.

## 249 CHURCH OF OUR LADY

Nørregade 8
Copenhagen K ①
+45 3315 1078
*www.domkirken.dk*

Completed in 1829, the neoclassical Vor Frue Kirke (Church of Our Lady) is the National Cathedral of Denmark and, in 2004, hosted the wedding of Frederik, Crown Prince of Denmark, and Mary Elizabeth Donaldson. One highlight of this church are the impressive sculptures lining the central nave, each created by the Danish sculptor Bertel Thorvaldsen.

## 250 CHURCH OF OUR SAVIOR

Sankt Annæ Gade 29
Christianshavn ②
+45 3254 6883
*www.vorfrelserskirke.dk*

With its impressive twisting black and gold spire reaching 90 metres above the street, the Baroque Church of Our Savior is a beloved landmark. Located along the canals of Christianshavn, the church is also well-known for its giant carillon bells, the largest in northern Europe, which toll everyday between 8 am and midnight. For a nominal fee, brave souls can climb to the top of the spire for one of the truly great views of the city.

# The 5 most impressive
# ROYAL BUILDINGS

251 **THE BLACK DIAMOND**
Søren Kierkegaards
Plads 1
Copenhagen K ⓘ
+45 3347 4747
*www.kb.dk*

Designed by Schmidt Hammer Lassen Architects, the new library wing's facade is crafted with polished black granite and glass and is just as impressive inside as it is outside. The library is open to the public.

252 **THE ROYAL DANISH PLAYHOUSE**
Sankt Annæ Plads 36
Copenhagen K ⓘ
+45 3369 6969
*www.kglteater.dk*

Overlooking Copenhagen Harbour, The Playhouse is a modern building with a generous waterfront terrace and an outdoor cafe and cocktail bar. Performance and Playhouse tour tickets are available at the box office.

253 **THE ROYAL DANISH THEATRE**
Kongens Nytorv 9
Copenhagen K ⓘ
+45 3369 6933
*www.kglteater.dk*

The Royal Danish Theatre has stood proudly at Kongens Nytorv since 1874 and is the current home to the renowned Royal Danish Ballet. Designed by the celebrated architect Vilhelm Dahlerup, the 1600-seat theatre hosts concerts, dramatic performances, and operas.

### 254 ROSENBORG CASTLE

Øster Voldgade 4A
Copenhagen K ⓘ
+45 3315 3286
www.kongernessamling.dk/
rosenborg

Built by King Christian IV, stately Rosenborg Castle was originally intended as a summer residence for the Danish royal family. Today, the Dutch Renaissance style castle overlooks one of the city's most popular public parks and houses the Throne Chair of Denmark as well as the Danish crown jewels.

### 255 AMALIENBORG PALACE

Amalienborg Slotsplads 5
Copenhagen K ⓘ
+45 3312 2186
www.kongernessamling.dk/
amalienborg

Originally designed and built as palaces for four different families, Amalienborg is, today, the winter home of Queen Margrethe II of Denmark. Situated on an architectural axis with the neighbouring Marble Church, Amalie Garden, and the extraordinary Royal Opera House across the harbour, Amalienborg is protected by the Royal Life Guards.

252 THE ROYAL DANISH PLAYHOUSE

# 5 icons of
# 20TH-CENTURY ARCHITECTURE

---

### 256 BELLA VISTA ESTATES
Strandvejen 419-433
Klampenborg ⑧

Built in 1934, the Bella Vista apartments were designed by Arne Jacobsen in an elegant modernist style and positioned to achieve maximum views toward the waters of the Øresund and to Sweden beyond. More than 80 years after being built, these flats are still some of the most exclusive in all of Copenhagen.

### 257 HOTEL ASTORIA
Banegårdspladsen 4
Copenhagen V ③

The Hotel Astoria, first opened in 1935, has long been an icon of modern functionalist architecture. Topped with a vintage Danish State Railway 'hood ornament', this unique piece of architectural history has recently been reopened as a boutique hotel.

### 258 FINN JUHL'S HOUSE
Kratvænget 15
Charlottenlund ⑧
+45 3964 1183

From the outside, the home of renowned Danish designer Finn Juhl is relatively unimpressive. According to Juhl's modernist vision, it was the details of interior spaces that were most important to any home. Juhl's home has been perfectly preserved and is open to the public.

## 259 SKOVSHOVED PETROL STATION

Kystvejen 24
Charlottenlund ⑧

Nicknamed 'the mushroom', Arne Jacobsen's 1938 minimalist seaside petrol station has stood the test of time. Originally developed as a prototype for a series of Texaco filling stations, the multi-station building plan never came to fruition, thus leaving the Skovshoved Petrol as a truly unique work.

## 260 KNIPPEL BRIDGE CONTROL TOWERS

connecting
Copenhagen Centre
to Christianshavn
Christianshavn ②

Named for 17th-century bridge keeper Hans Knip, the green Knippelbro (Knippel Bridge) control towers are Copenhagen landmarks. Standing sentry at both ends of the drawbridge that spans Copenhagen's inner harbour, the control towers, designed by Kaj Gottlob, even show up on Danish 200-kroner banknote.

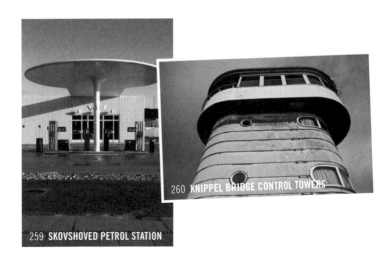

260 KNIPPEL BRIDGE CONTROL TOWERS

259 SKOVSHOVED PETROL STATION

# The 5 most stunning examples of
# NEW DANISH ARCHITECTURE

---

**261 TIETGEN STUDENT HALL**
Rued Langgaards Vej 10
Copenhagen S ⑦

Envisioned as the student 'dormitory of the future', this cylindrical, seven-storey student housing complex was designed by Lundgaard & Tranberg Architects. Completed in 2006, Tietgen Student Hall has become a case study in effective residential design and is home to around 400 students at any given time. The Student Hall can usually be admired from the outside only.

**262 CIS NORDHAVN**
Levantkaj Vest
Inner Nordhavn
Copenhagen Ø ⑤

At the heart of the Nordhavn redevelopment is the new 25.000-square-metre waterfront campus of Copenhagen International School (CIS), designed by C.F. Møller Architects and set for completion in 2016. The new CIS will be clad in over 12.000 solar panels that will help to make it one of the most innovative and energy-efficient school buildings in the world.

**263 8 HOUSE**
Richard Mortensens Vej
Copenhagen S ⑦
*www.stallet.dk*

At, literally, the southernmost tip of Copenhagen's Ørestad district is the ambitious 'bow tie shaped' 8 House, a mixed use development designed by Danish architects BIG (Bjarke Ingels Group).

## 264 THE ROYAL DANISH OPERA HOUSE

Ekvipagemestervej 10
Christianshavn ②
+45 3369 6969
*www.kglteater.dk*

Located just across the water from the royal residence of the Queen of Denmark, the Royal Opera House has become the city's most recognizable architectural icon. Built in 2004/2005, the new 1400-seat Opera House was designed by Danish architect Henning Larsen and features light sculptures by Icelandic sculptor Olafur Eliasson.

## 265 MOUNTAIN DWELLINGS

Ørestads Boulevard 55
Copenhagen S ⑦

Another urban triumph from the team at Denmark's BIG Architects, the Mountain Dwellings development in Ørestad is 2/3 parking block and 1/3 housing block. The housing units are built atop the sloping concrete parking structure, thus allowing for an artificial mountainside below and cascading, terraced apartments high above street level.

264 THE ROYAL DANISH OPERA HOUSE

## 5 good reasons to visit the
# DANISH ARCHITECTURE CENTRE

---

DAC
Strandgade 27B
Christianshavn ②
+45 3257 1930
www.dac.dk

266 **BECOME AN ARCHITECTURE EXPERT**

Danish architecture and design is known and respected worldwide and the exhibitions inside the Copenhagen's DAC is the best place to become an expert in Denmark's rich design tradition, architectural eras and movements, recent trends, and most famous personalities.

267 **ARCHITECTURE TOURS**

Every Sunday, the Danish Architecture Centre offers English language tours around Copenhagen (during the summer months) and within the DAC's current exhibits (all year), both of which are great ways to get a deeper understanding of the who, what, and when, where, and why of Danish architecture.

268 **COFFEE WITH THE BEST VIEW IN TOWN**

Looking over the water and back toward the city centre, the DAC& CAFE has, unquestionably, one of the very best views in the city. In addition, the cafe's food recently received a 5 out of 6 star rating by the Danish newspaper *Politiken*. Tip: come for the weekend brunch served Saturday and Sunday from 11 am till 5 pm.

269 **ACTIVITIES FOR KIDS OF ALL AGES**

Every Sunday, the DAC offers family-friendly workshops with themes corresponding to one of the centre's current exhibitions. Whether building with LEGO or drawing with pencils and colours, these workshops are hands-on learning opportunities for kids of all ages.

270 **A CURATED GIFT SHOP**

If you're looking to bring home unique gifts for the design-lover in your life, the DAC's beautifully curated gift shop has a variety of handpicked Danish design products to choose from, as well as Northern Europe's largest selection of architecture and design-related books.

CHRISTIANSHAVN

# 75 PLACES TO DISCOVER COPENHAGEN

---

## 5 best places to
# HIRE A BICYCLE

---

**271 BAISIKELI**
Ingerslevsgade 80
Copenhagen V ③
+45 2670 0229
*www.baisikeli.dk*

Baisikeli is a bike repair and hire shop doing some real good in the world – the shop's name means 'bicycle' in Swahili. The team at Baisikeli collects used bicycles in Denmark and sends them to Africa, where secondhand bikes help to generate jobs, promote education, and provide personal transportation.

**272 CYKELBØRSEN**
Gothersgade 157
Copenhagen K ①
+45 3314 0717
*www.cykelborsen.dk*

Since 1881, Cykelbørsen (the bicycle exchange) has been a respected name in the business of bicycle sales, repairs, and rentals. The shop's founder supposedly helped to teach over 2000 people to ride a bike during his life.

**273 BIKE RENTAL COPENHAGEN**
Kongens Nytorv 8
Copenhagen K ①
+45 3082 0095
*www.bikerental copenhagen.dk*

Located at Kongens Nytorv, in the very heart of the city, Bike Rental Copenhagen keeps it simple with only three bike options to choose from. The convenient location for pick-up and drop-off makes this shop a good option for those staying in the city centre. Tip: book ahead online and receive a 20% discount.

## 274 BYCYKLEN

Bredgade 36B
Copenhagen K ⓘ
+45 8988 3910
www.bycyklen.dk

The white, pay-as-you-go Bycyklen (City Cycles) are available for hire at locations throughout the city. In order to hire or reserve a Bycyclen, you will need a user account (set up online with an email address and a credit card). The City Cycles are each equipped with an electric motor and built-in locks, lights, and luggage rack.

## 275 COPENHAGEN BICYCLES

Nyhavn 44
Copenhagen K ⓘ
+45 3393 0404

If you hire from Copenhagen Bicycles, you can join the shop's daily guided bike tour of Copenhagen for only 100 additional kroner. All bikes come with lock and lights.

271 BAISIKELI

*The 5 most charming*

# NEIGHBOURHOODS TO EXPLORE

---

276 **BRUMLEBY**
between Øster Allé and
Østerbrogade
Copenhagen Ø ⑤

The miniature yellow city of Brumleby, built in the 1850s, is an early example of Danish social housing. Founded by a group of physicians during the Copenhagen cholera epidemic of 1853, Brumleby is now protected as a historic city landmark. Tip: this is still an active (and friendly) community, so when you visit remember to respect the residents' privacy.

277 **OLUFSVEJ**
Copenhagen Ø ⑤

Just around the corner from Brumleby is a single street of brightly coloured row houses facing each other across a street. Usually local kids are playing and neighbours are chatting on their terraces. Unlike Brumleby, the original owners of the houses on Olufsvej were mostly artisans, clerks, and merchants.

276 **BRUMLEBY**

278 SKOVSHOVED

## 278 SKOVSHOVED

Strandvejen 267
Charlottenlund ⑧

The charming fishing village of Skovshoved, with roots dating back to the 13th century, is located north of Copenhagen and immediately west of the newly-expanded Skovshoved Harbour. The wives of the area's fishermen are famous for having carried each day's catch on their backs all the way to Copenhagen's markets, 11 kilometres away. Today, many of the historic thatch-roofed cottages and narrow village streets remain.

## 279 NYBODER

located between Store
Kongensgade, Øster
Voldgade and Sankt
Pauls Gade
Copenhagen K ①

First developed by King Christian IV in the 17th century, the ochre-coloured buildings of Nyboder (new small houses) were originally built as barracks for the Royal Navy. Mostly unchanged since the 18th century, the iconic neighbourhood of Nyboder has been featured in the creative works of both Søren Kierkegaard and Hans Christian Andersen.

## 280 FARIMAGSGADE DISTRICT

between Øster Søgade
and Øster Farimagsgade
Copenhagen K ①

Consisting of nearly 500 terraced 'potato row' houses built in the 1870s, the English-style homes of the Farimagsgade District were originally built to provide healthy housing for the city's poor. Today, these charming lakeside homes are some of the most desirable in Copenhagen's centre.

## *The 5 best*
# VIEWS FROM ABOVE
## *the city*

---

### 281 THE ROUND TOWER

Købmagergade 52A
Copenhagen K ①
+45 3373 0373

Originally built as an astronomical observatory, the Rundetårn (the Round Tower) is one of the most unassuming and overlooked treasures in the city. For a very small fee, visitors can enter the 17th-century tower and ascend the spiral ramp, originally designed for horses to climb, toward the observatory at the top. It's not an easy hike up, but the views from the top are well worth the effort.

### 282 CHRISTIANSBORG PALACE TOWER

Prins Jørgens Gård 1
Copenhagen K ①
+45 3392 6492

Known as 'Borgen' by locals, Christians-borg Palace was once the main residence of the Danish royalty but is now the home of the Danish Parliament. For decades, the Christiansborg Tower, which stands 106 metres high, was off limits, but finally opened to the public in 2014. Lucky for you, there's a lift to the top of the tower, and, best of all, admission is free.

## 283 SKY BAR & RESTAURANT
### AT BELLA SKY HOTEL

Center Boulevard 5
Copenhagen S ⑦
+45 3247 3000
www.acbellasky
copenhagen.dk

What's classier than enjoying a glass of champagne 75 metres above street level, while taking in a view over the sea toward Sweden? Not much. Now open for lunch as well as dinner and drinks, the ultra-classy Sky Bar & Restaurant is a stylish way to take in a stunning view as well as a world-class meal.

## 284 STAR FLYER
### AT TIVOLI GARDENS

Vesterbrogade 3
Copenhagen K ①
+45 3315 1001
www.tivoli.dk

The iconic Tivoli Gardens are beloved for their beautiful landscape design, vintage charm, and extravagant seasonal decorations. But, high above the park, dangling and swinging from the Star Flyer – the highest carousel in Northern Europe – is the only place to get a high-speed, 360-degree tour of Copenhagen.

## 285 STICKS'N'SUSHI
### AT THE TIVOLI HOTEL

Arni Magnussons Gade 2
Copenhagen V ③
+45 4487 0000
www.tivolihotel.com

Offering stunning views in both rain or sunshine, the Sticks'n'Sushi restaurant atop the Lego-like Tivoli Hotel is a favourite 'special occasion' dining destination for locals. From the rooftop restaurant's breathtaking vantage point, the entire bustling life of the capital can be observed below.

# *The 5 best*
# **DAY TRIPS**
# *from Copenhagen*

286 **DRAGØR**
   Denmark

Located just outside of Copenhagen, this historic fishing village is a photographer's dream: yellow thatch-roofed cottages, crooked streets, hidden passageways, quaint seaside cafes, and a scenic harbor dating back to at least the 14th century. And, if the weather is fine when you visit, make sure to take advantage of Dragør's cosy beach as well.

287 **HVEN**
   Sweden

Only one hour from Copenhagen by ferry, Hven is a small and isolated Swedish island, crisscrossed by bike paths and dotted with quaint seaside villages, churches, and lighthouses. Rent a bike, tour the towns, and stop by the exquisite Backafallsbyn whisky bar before taking the evening ferry back to Copenhagen.

## 288 MØNS KLINT (THE CLIFFS OF MØN)

Island of Møn
Denmark

Steep, stark white, and impressive, Møns Klint is a highlight of the otherwise subtle Danish landscape. These chalk cliffs stand as one of the highest points of elevation in Denmark and their environs are protected as a nature park, popular with cyclists, hikers, campers, and amateur geologists. In the summer months, visitors can access Møns Klint via bus from Copenhagen.

## 289 BORNHOLM

Denmark

Known to many as 'the sunny island', Bornholm is probably best experienced as a two or three day trip from Copenhagen, but technically it can be done in a single day. Known for its lovely weather, water sports, artisanal boutiques, and laidback lifestyle, Bornholm is a beloved getaway for Copenhageners.

## 290 LOUISIANA MUSEUM OF MODERN ART

Gammel Strandvej 13
Humlebæk
Denmark
+45 4919 0719
www.louisiana.dk

A short train ride up the coast from Copenhagen is the quiet seaside town of Humlebæk, home to the Louisiana Museum of Modern Art. Since opening in 1958, Louisiana has been almost as famous for its architecture and setting – overlooking the sea – as it is for its international collections of artwork. Tip: when visiting Louisiana, take some time to explore the historic fishing village of Sletten, just a short walk away.

## *The 5 best local*
# BEACHES AND SWIMMING SPOTS

---

**291 BELLEVUE BEACH**
Strandvejen 340
Klampenborg ⑧

North of the city centre and just a few steps from Klampenborg train station is fashionable Bellevue Beach. Featuring 700 metres of sand, Arne Jacobsen watch towers, and a reputation for attracting nude sunbathers, Bellevue epitomizes the classic 'Danish Riviera' beach experience.

**292 HARBOUR BATH**
Islands Brygge 7
Copenhagen S ②

Located in the very heart of Copenhagen, Islands Brygge is an essential swimming spot for locals. With views of the city, a grassy lawn for lounging and barbecues, and the best diving platform in town, Harbour Bath is the best of summer in the city. The baths are open in June, July, and August.

## 293 **KASTRUP SEA BATH**
Amager Strandvej 301
Kastrup ⑦

In winter, the Kastrup Sea Bath is an architectural curiosity: an uninhabited, curling wooden seashell hovering out over the water between Denmark and Sweden. But in the summer, the Sea Bath is a gathering place for local sunbathers, swimmers, and daredevils who come to take the plunge off the bath's 3- and 5-metre jumping platforms.

## 294 **AMAGER BEACH PARK**
Amager Strandvej 110
Copenhagen S ⑦

Unlike anything else in Copenhagen, the Amager Beach Park area is a diverse and semi-wild getaway from the city that features wide beaches, grassy lawns, sports facilities, sand dunes and access to numerous waterfront activities. The Beach Park is easily accessed from Copenhagen via the Metro line M2.

## 295 **CHARLOTTENLUND BEACH**
Strandvejen 150
Charlottenlund ⑧

On the east side of Charlottenlund Fort is a narrow strip of park and sandy beach almost completely hidden from the noise and traffic of the adjacent and busy main coastal road. And this quiet isolation is what makes Charlottenlund Beach such a beloved hidden gem for locals. Come to explore the fort, for a swim, or to admire the sailboats from nearby Skovshoved harbour.

291 **BELLEVUE BEACH**

# The 5 best places to
## PEOPLE WATCH

---

**296 NYHAVN**
Copenhagen K ⓘ

There is no better place in Copenhagen to take in the parade of humans than at Nyhavn, the city's most well-visited area. Here you can either settle in at one of the cafes on Nyhavn's north side or find a place on the quieter south bank.

**297 AMAGERTORV**
Copenhagen K ⓘ

At this busy pedestrian-only crossroads, the city's two main shopping streets meet and connect some of the capital's most important places. Recommended: a seat on the terrace (or at the window) of Cafe Europa 1989.

**298 ISRAELS PLADS**
Copenhagen K ⓘ

Named in honour of Denmark's Jewish community, the recently redesigned Israels Plads is an innovative urban park that's almost always thronging with life. Whether busy with basketball players, skater kids, or antique dealers, Israels Plads is an ideal place to enjoy some takeaway from the nearby Torvehallerne and do some people watching.

### 299 FREDERIKSBERG GARDENS

Frederiksberg
Runddel 1A
Frederiksberg ⑥
+45 3395 4200

The spacious Frederiksberg Gardens have a little something for everyone: a zoo, playgrounds, rowboats on the lake, a Swiss cottage, a miniature Roman temple, and a real Danish palace. But, it's the wide open lawns of the park that are best for people watching.

### 300 CITY HALL SQUARE

Copenhagen K ①

Just steps away from the ever-popular Tivoli Gardens and the city's central train station, there is an endless stream of crowds passing through the City Hall Square both day and night.

296 **NYHAVN**

# *The 5 most lovely*
# **PARKS**
## *near the city centre*

301 **BOTANICAL GARDENS**
Øster Farimagsgade 2B
Copenhagen K ⓘ
+45 3532 2222

The Botanical Gardens are a delightful convergence of outdoor science lab, city park, and adventure space. Featuring over 13.000 species of plantlife laid out over ten rambling hectares, this is a great place to wander. During your visit, make sure to visit the impressive 19th-century glass Palm House.

302 **ROYAL LIBRARY GARDEN**
Søren Kierkegaards
Plads 1
Copenhagen K ⓘ
+45 3395 4200

Nestled between the Danish Parliament building and the Royal Library, and hidden by a tall stone wall, the elegant and often overlooked Royal Library Garden is an excellent place to enjoy a takeaway lunch or just to sit and read a while.

303 **ØRSTEDSPARKEN**
Nørre Voldgade 1
Copenhagen K ⓘ

Ørstedparken's rolling hills, massive trees, and central lake create the effect of a natural woodland but it is the dozens of monuments and classical sculptures that make this park so distinct and whimsical.

### 304 ROSENBORG CASTLE GARDENS

Gothersgade 11
Copenhagen K ⓘ
+45 3395 4200

This popular city park has it all: a Renaissance castle, a formal rose garden, wide open lawns as well as stylish cafes along the perimeter. Commonly known as Kongen's Have (King's Garden), this is the spot Copenhageners flock to when the sun comes out.

### 305 THE CITADEL

Gl. Hovedvagt
Kastellet 1
Copenhagen K ⓘ

At the intersection of Østerbro and central Copenhagen is the historic military citadel known locally as Kastellet. Now preserved as a public park, Kastellet's outer ring of shady atmospheric green spaces as well as its brighter interior areas are both popular with runners and urban ramblers.

305 THE CITADEL

# The 5 best
# ANNUAL EVENTS
## to attend

---

### 306 CHRISTMAS
#### AT TIVOLI GARDENS
Vesterbrogade 3
Copenhagen K ①
+45 3315 1001
*www.tivoli.dk*

For six weeks every year, the historic Tivoli Gardens transforms from a sunny amusement park into a magical winter wonderland. Complete with Christmas lights, traditional food stalls, gift markets, Danish mulled wine, holiday concerts, and even Father Christmas, Christmas at Tivoli is the perfect holiday experience for children of all ages.

### 307 SANKTHANS AFTEN

Sankthans is a national holiday originally founded to celebrate the feast of St. John the Baptist. In past times, it was thought that Denmark's witches would come out and fly on the night of the solstice, and so it became common for communities to light large bonfires around the country to scare the witches away. Today, Danes celebrate Sankthans every June – near midsummer's eve – with beach parties, long family dinners, and, of course, bonfires.

### 308 CPH:DOX
*cphdox.dk*

CPH:DOX is the third largest documentary film festival in the world. Since 2003, this expanding festival has filled Copenhagen's cinemas with a selection of more than 200 films from around the world. The CPH:DOX festival programme also features concerts, industry gatherings, lectures, and art exhibitions.

### 309 COPENHAGEN KULTURNATTEN
*www.kulturnatten.dk*

For one night in October, the city of Copenhagen creates a vast programme of cultural opportunities open to the public. And while many museums and government buildings are open for tours and lectures, this event is most beloved for the unusual, entertaining, and uniquely odd events that only happen once per year on *Kulturnatten* (Culture Night): 'human tower' building, midnight swimming, graveyard ghost walks, and cadaver displays.

### 310 NORTHMODERN, FURNITURE AND LIFE-STYLE TRADE SHOW
*www.northmodern.com*

Founded in 2015, the successful northmodern trade show is an open 'celebration of holistic, sustainable contemporary living'. This design-centric event brings together the many strands of creative industries currently thriving in the Nordic region into one-of-a-kind experience for professionals, aspiring makers, and design enthusiasts. Held twice per year.

# 5 recognizable places from
# NORDIC NOIR TV

311 **JESUS CHURCH**
Kirkevænget 5A
Valby ⑥
+45 3630 3579
*www.jesuskirken.dk*

The unusual, Italianate Jesus Church in Valby was commissioned by Carlsberg beer magnate Carl Jacobsen, whose family is now buried in the church's crypt. Jesus Church was used for funeral scenes in the popular Danish TV series *Borgen* (2010-2013). Tip: don't miss the statue *Troll that smells Christian blood*.

312 **COPENHAGEN POLICE HEADQUARTERS**
Politigården
Copenhagen V ③
+45 3314 1448

Once considered a masterpiece of the stark neoclassical style of European architecture, Copenhagen's Politigården (police headquarters) was built in 1924 and is well known to viewers of *The Bridge, The Killing*, and several other popular Danish crime series.

313 **HUMLEBY NEIGHBOURHOOD**
Ernst Meyers Gade
Copenhagen V ③
*www.humleby.dk*

This yellow bricked 'city within the city' was built in the 1880s as housing for the employees of Burmeister & Wain, a large industrial manufacturer. Located just outside of Vesterbro, the charming neighbourhood of Humleby shows up in several episodes of the Danish series *The Killing* (2007-2012).

314 **ØRESUND BRIDGE**

Opened in July of 2000, the Øresund Bridge is the principal road and rail connection between Copenhagen and Malmo, Sweden. The elegant profile of the bridge can be viewed from both countries and was a central setting in the first series of the Danish-Swedish crime series *The Bridge* (2011-present).

315 **THE DANISH PARLIAMENT**

Christiansborg Slot 1
Copenhagen K ①
+45 3337 3221

The *Borgen* TV series takes its title from the nickname of Christiansborg, the stately home to the Danish parliament, the Danish constitution, and the prime minister's offices. Tip: check online for the schedule of free, English language tours of Christiansborg offered throughout the year.

312 COPENHAGEN POLICE HEADQUARTERS

## The 5 best reasons to visit
# FREETOWN CHRISTIANIA

---

**316 THE NATURAL BEAUTY**

Most people who have heard of Christiania know it as a hippie commune created back in the early 1970s. Many people know it as the centre of Copenhagen's counterculture community as well as a place where hashish is traded and consumed openly, though technically illegal. But what a lot of people are not aware of is how lovely the area's nature is, especially the lake, the canal, and the surrounding woods.

**317 ARCHITECTURE WITHOUT ARCHITECTS**

Another reason to explore Christiania is the quirky, freeform residential architecture of the Freetown's family homes. Most of these houses were built with found materials by the residents themselves - or past residents - and are unlike any other houses in Copenhagen. Remember to be respectful of the residents and their privacy.

319 THE WOMEN METALSMITH'S WORKSHOP

## 318 A MEAL AT CAFE NEMOLAND

Fabriksområdet 52
Christianshavn ②
+45 3295 8931
*www.nemoland.dk*

The large open air music venue, cafe, and beer garden known as Nemoland is the best place in Christiania to sit back and enjoy some good, old fashioned people watching. The mostly organic food here is surprisingly excellent and the overall vibe is friendly, relaxed, and inclusive. Tip: share a picnic table, introduce yourself, and make a new friend or two.

## 319 THE WOMEN METAL-SMITH'S WORKSHOP AND GALLERY

Mælkevejen 83E
Christianshavn ②
+45 3257 7658
*www.kvindesmedien.dk*

For almost two decades, the Kvindesmedien (the Women Metalsmiths) has been one of the most acclaimed of Christiania's working art studios. The three women who run the metalshop (Dorte Eilenberger, Charlotte Steen and Gitte Christensen) are each celebrated artists in their own right and have had their works displayed in major galleries.

## 320 ANOTHER SIDE OF COPENHAGEN

Spending an afternoon in Christiania may not be for everyone; especially if you are sensitive to open drug use, graffiti covered walls, and / or the presence of free roaming cats and dogs. But what most visitors appreciate about this area is the startling and colourful contrast between Christiania and the rest of the otherwise straight-laced Danish capital. Note: the area is generally safe, but always exercise caution and do not take photos on or around Pusher Street.

*The 5 most interesting*

# GRAVES IN ASSISTENS KIRKEGÅRD

Kapelvej 4
Copenhagen N ④
+45 3537 1917

321 **NIELS BOHR**
(1885-1962)

As the most important Danish scientist of the 20th century, Bohr was a key figure in the development of modern theoretical physics, quantum theory, and nuclear energy. Bohr helped the allies develop The Manhattan Project and, after WWII, helped establish the CERN laboratory in Switzerland.

322 **BEN WEBSTER**
(1909-1973)

American jazz legend Ben Webster worked with some of the greatest jazz musicians of all time: Duke Ellington, Coleman Hawkins, Art Tatum, and many others. He spent the last years of his life in Copenhagen and, since his death, his annual royalties go to support jazz music in Denmark.

### 323 GIERTRUD BIRGITTE BODENHOFF
(1779-1798)

Every cemetery has at least one ghost story, and the ghost of Assistens Kirkegård may very well be Giertrud Bodenhoff. Married at age 17, widowed at age 19, legend claims – and modern investigations support – that, under anesthesia, Giertrud was accidentally buried alive in 1798, only to be awakened and murdered by grave robbers.

### 324 HANS CHRISTIAN ØRSTED
(1777-1851)

The second most famous Hans Christian buried in Assistens Kirkegård, H.C. Ørsted was the Danish poet-scientist who discovered electromagnetism in the 1820s. Ørsted's law – the scientific principle explaining the relationship between electric currents and magnetic fields – honors his legacy.

### 325 JACOB MILLING
(1863-1912)

En route to the United States to study railroad production, the Danish engineer Jacob Milling died when the Titanic sank on April 15, 1912. The body of the 48-year-old husband and father was later recovered and sent back to Copenhagen to be laid to rest in Assistens Kirkegård.

ASSISTENS KIRKEGÅRD

## The 5 best places for
# COPENHAGEN PRIDE

---

**326  COPENHAGEN CITY HALL**
Rådhuspladsen 1
Copenhagen K ①
+45 3366 2585
*www.kk.dk*

In 1989, Denmark became the first country in the world to legally recognize same-sex registered partnerships. On October 1st of that year, Danish gay rights activists Axel Lundahl-Madsen and Eigil Eskildsen were married, along with ten other couples, at Copenhagen's *rådhus*. As of 2012, it has became legal for Danish State Churches to perform same-sex weddings.

**327  CAFE INTIME**
Allegade 25
Frederiksberg ⑥
+45 3834 1958
*www.cafeintime.dk*

Cafe Intime has been known as a gay-friendly bar since the early 1920s. This elegant, jazz-era piano bar is a classic gay-friendly destination and is open every evening until 2 am. Cafe Intime hosts numerous events throughout the week, including drag shows and live jazz every Sunday.

### 328 JAILHOUSE CPH

Studiestræde 12
Copenhagen K ①
+45 3315 2255
www.jailhousecph.dk

This quirky, 'prison-themed' gay bar and restaurant is a one of a kind. And with the bar staff dressed as guards, daily happy hours (3 pm - 9 pm), and regular special events (quiz nights, ABBA night, sailor's night, etc.) these guys aren't afraid of having a great time.

### 329 VELA GAY CLUB

Viktoriagade 2
Copenhagen V ③
+45 3331 3419
www.velagayclub.dk

One of Copenhagen's few lesbian clubs, Vela is a vibrant gathering place with a busy schedule of events: from table football, to guest DJs, to poetry nights, and regular live music, there's always a party at Vela. Tip: no cocktails here, at Vela they're known as 'pussytails'.

### 330 COPENHAGEN PRIDE WEEK

Organized and operated entirely by volunteers, the mission of Copenhagen Pride is to help make the LGBT community in Copenhagen more visible and better represented. Each August, Copenhagen Pride Week draws large crowds of LGBT community members and supporters to the event's Pride Square gathering and for the festive Pride Week parade through the city.

## *The 5 most inspiring*
# URBAN DETAILS

**331 THE CHANGING OF THE ROYAL LIFE GUARDS**

The changing of the Danish Royal Life Guards is one of the most celebrated and charming events in the daily life of Copenhagen. Each day the new guard departs their barracks at Rosenborg Castle at precisely 11.27 am and marches via one of various routes through the city centre to the Royal Palace of Amalienborg in time to arrive for the 12 pm (noon) changing of the guard.

**332 SUNRISE AND SUNSET CANNON SALUTE**

The historic military battery of King Christian VI is located just across Copenhagen Harbour from the city's infamous *The Little Mermaid* statue. And every day, at sunrise and sunset, soldiers at Battery Sixtus fire a cannon salute to accompany the official raising and lowering of the fort's *Dannebrog* (the Danish flag). Depending on where you are in the city centre – and on the direction of the wind – you can hear the cannon fire every day of the year.

## 333 COPENHAGEN BIKE COUNTERS

Copenhagen has established electronic bicycle counters at several locations throughout the city. These counters help the city planners monitor trends in bike use and the easiest bike counter to find is located on Dronning Louise's bridge, which crosses the Copenhagen lakes and is part of the most-biked route in all of Denmark.

## 334 CYCLE SNAKE BRIDGE

West Entrance at
Kalvebod Brygge 59
Copenhagen V ③

Winding through the air above Copen-hagen's inner harbour, the 230-metre-long Cycle Snake is a bicycle-only sky bridge that acts as a shortcut, connecting the Islands Brygge district to busy Vesterbro. Designed by DISSING+WEITLING architecture, the brightly painted Cycle Snake is used by more than 12.000 cyclists every day and is a must-experience for cycle enthusiasts.

## 335 FREE BOOK EXCHANGES

At five different locations in Copenhagen's Gentofte district, north of the city, you can find freestanding, outdoor *bogbørsen* (book exchanges). These 3-metre tall, glass-wrapped bookcases often include English language books and anyone is free to give or take from the book exchange. The easiest *bogbørsen* to find is located near the intersection of Ahlmanns Allé and Duntzfelts Allé in Hellerup.

# The 5 most
# FASCINATING RELICS
## from Copenhagen's past

---

336 **THE HULDREMOSE WOMAN**
Denmark's National Museum
Ny Vestergade 10
Copenhagen K ⓘ
+45 3313 4411
*www.natmus.dk*

Discovered in western Denmark in 1879, this mummified Iron Age relic is one of the treasures of the National Museum in Copenhagen. Perfectly preserved in a low-oxygen bog for 2000 years, the Huldremose Woman was discovered wearing elaborate, well-preserved clothing made of leather and wool.

337 **TREKRONER SEA FORTRESS**
Trekroner 1
Copenhagen K ⓘ
+45 7242 4333
*www.trekronerfort.dk*

Trekroner Sea Fortress is an artificial island built back in 1713 to protect Copenhagen from naval attacks. Today it is a popular waterfront destination during the sunny days of summer. Reach the fortress via ferry from Nyhavn, from May through September.

338 **THE VICTORIAN HOME**
Frederiksholms Kanal 18
Copenhagen K ⓘ
+45 3313 4411
*www.natmus.dk*

The interiors of this unique, protected piece of Copenhagen's domestic history have been preserved almost exactly as they were between 1890 and 1914. You will see extraordinary examples of antique textiles, furniture, lighting, and decoration from the period.

### 339 BØRSEN

Børsgade 1
Copenhagen K ①
+45 3374 6000
*www.borsbygningen.dk*

Built in 1640, King Christian IV's Stock Exchange has survived numerous area fires and violent sieges of the city. The secret to this relic's longevity may be its 56-metre tall dragontail spire, which local legend says protects Børsen from destruction.

### 340 THE TUBORG BOTTLE

Dessaus Boulevard 4
Hellerup ⑧

Founded in 1873, Tuborg was the longtime rival of Carlsberg beer, until, in 1970, the two Danish breweries merged. Today, a 26-metre tall Tuborg beer bottle stands at the edge of the old brewery lands in Hellerup. It was originally built as an observation tower.

# *The 5 most charmingly*
# COLOURFUL STREETS
# & SQUARES

---

### 341 GRÅBRØDRETORV
Copenhagen K ①

Entering the extravagantly colourful Gråbrødretorv (Gray Brothers Square) from the intersection of Niels Hemmingsens Gade and Løvstræde provides the most impressive introduction to this cosy urban oasis. Whether in the dim days of winter or the long days of Danish summer, this quiet square is one of the most beautiful and overlooked in the city.

### 342 WILDERSGADE
Christianshavn ②

Whether biking over Knippelsbro Bridge into Christianshavn or arriving from Christianshavn Metro station, Wildersgade is a great place to discover some quaint, historic architecture. Bookended by Christianshavn Canal, the south end of Wildersgade is a mixture of old and modern buildings, but the area north of Torvegade has a quintessentially quirky and colourful Copenhagen vibe.

### 343 PISTOLSTRÆDE
Copenhagen K ⓘ

There are a few ways to enter the hidden street of Pistolstræde, but the best is by way of the alley-like entrance on Ny Østergade, very near to the main shopping street and Kongens Nytorv. Look for the archway announcing Pistolstræde (between Ny Østergade #9 and #11), opposite of Cafe Victor.

### 344 STUDIESTRÆDE
Copenhagen K ⓘ

Studiestræde (Study Street) stretches from the Copenhagen cathedral at its north end to Copenhagen's theatre district (near Vesterport station) to the south. Make sure to take your time and notice the diversity of Studiestræde's businesses, buildings, courtyards, and people.

### 345 LARSBJØRNSSTRÆDE
Copenhagen K ⓘ

Larsbjørnsstræde is a colourful pedestrian street lined with a wide variety of bars, boutiques and cafes. It changes names a few times along its length. Tip: as you travel south down Larsbjørnsstræde from Ørsted's Park, make sure to turn left onto Kompagnistræde, another of the centre's most interesting streets of architectural curios.

# 40 PLACES
# TO ENJOY CULTURE

———

# The 5 best places for
# STREET ART

### 346 PEACE 69
**Jagtvej 69**
**Copenhagen N** ④

In the summer of 2011, American street artist Shepard Fairey created three large street art murals in Copenhagen: the controversial *Peace 69* at Jagtvej 69 in Nørrebro, a piece titled *Guns and Roses* on Nygårdsvej in Østerbro, and a mural celebrating Arab women near Dybbølsbro train station. Today, only *Peace 69* – though vandalized – remains.

### 347 WESTEND PASSAGE
**between Vesterbrogade**
**65 and 67**
**Copenhagen V** ③

Located immediately off of the busy thoroughfare of Vesterbrogade is the tiny arched tunnel of Westend Passage, which leads through to the quiet neighbourhood of Westend. Every three to five weeks an artist reclaims the passage walls and covers them with his or her own vision, creating an ever-changing gallery of street art.

### 348 SUPERKILEN URBAN PARK
**Heimdalsgade**
**Copenhagen N** ④

*Superkilen* is an ambitious and award-winning project made up of three distinct parts: the red square, the black market, and the green park. The goal of the project is to celebrate the diversity of northern Copenhagen, where more than 50 nationalities are known to live, and invite the different communities to come together.

### 349 KONGENS NYTORV METRO BUILDING SITE
Kongens Nytorv
Copenhagen K ①

The green walls surrounding the Metro building site at Kongens Nytorv, in the city centre, have hosted numerous impressive and interactive art installations. These installations are changing frequently, so just stop by to see what's new.

### 350 V1 GALLERY
Flæsketorvet 69-71
Copenhagen V ③
+45 3331 0321
www.v1gallery.com

Founded in 2002, V1 Gallery is the kind of space where all kinds of art, including the stylings of street art, are celebrated and used as a jumping off point for social, political, and cultural discussion. The emphasis is on young creatives with an urban sensibility.

350 V1 GALLERY

# The 5 most inspiring
# ART MUSEUMS

351 **ORDRUPGAARD**
Vilvordevej 110
Charlottenlund ⑧
+45 3964 1183
*www.ordrupgaard.dk*

Originally built as a private residence in the woods, Ordrupgaard now includes a stunning addition designed by architect Zaha Hadid. The heart of the museum's permanent collection includes works by Degas, Renoir, Monet, Cézanne, Gauguin, and Matisse. Paid admission includes access to the preserved home of Danish architect Finn Juhl.

352 **HIRSCHSPRUNG COLLECTION**
Stockholmsgade 20
Copenhagen Ø ⑤
+45 3542 0336
*www.hirschsprung.dk*

The Hirschsprung Collection celebrates Danish art from the 19th and early 20th centuries. This intimate museum, situated in Østre Anlæg park, includes works from the Danish Golden Age through to the early modern period.

353 **ARKEN MUSEUM OF MODERN ART**
Skovvej 100
Ishøj ⑧
+45 4354 0222
*www.arken.dk*

The impressive ARKEN Museum of Modern Art is located on Køge Bay Beach in Ishøj, just south of Copenhagen. ARKEN's permanent collection emphasises modern Danish, Nordic, and international art from after 1990, including works by Ai Weiwei, Damien Hirst and Olafur Eliasson.

### 354 THORVALDSENS MUSEUM

Bertel Thorvaldsens
Plads 2
Copenhagen K ①
+45 3332 1532
*www.thorvaldsens
museum.dk*

The collection in this museum concentrates on the life's work of one man, Danish master sculptor Bertel Thorvaldsen (1770-1844), who donated his entire body of work to the city of Copenhagen in 1838. Tip: admission is free on Wednesdays.

### 355 KUNSTHAL CHARLOTTENBORG

Kongens Nytorv 1
Copenhagen K ①
+45 3374 4639
*www.kunsthal
charlottenborg.dk*

This historic palace is home to one of the most overlooked art spaces in Copenhagen, the Charlottenborg Art Hall, the official exhibition gallery of the Royal Danish Academy of Art. The museum's cafe and bookshop are also well worth a visit.

351 ORDRUPGAARD

352 HIRSCHSPRUNG COLLECTION

357 CARL JACOBSEN'S COLLECTION OF ANCIENT ART

# 5 good reasons to visit the
# NY CARLSBERG GLYPTOTEK

---

Dantes Plads 7
Copenhagen K ①
+45 3341 8141
*www.glyptoteket.com*

356 **THE ARCHITECTURE**

The Ny Carlsberg Glyptotek has a truly impressive collection, but also the museum building itself is one of Copenhagen's most celebrated works of historical architecture.

357 **NORTHERN EUROPE'S LARGEST COLLECTION OF ANCIENT ART**

Carlsberg brewing magnate Carl Jacobsen spent his life assembling the collection of art that is now housed in The Glyptotek. A collection that has grown to over 10.000 items since Jacobsen's death in 1914, with priceless items originating from ancient Egypt, Greece, and Italy (among others).

## 358 THE WINTER GARDEN & CAFÉ GLYPTOTEKET

Located between the Glyptotek's two main buildings is the museum's glass-domed, palm-lined Winter Garden. And, no matter what the weather is doing outside, this magical space somehow always feels like a tropical oasis. The Winter Garden is also home to the museum's cafe.

## 359 THE EUROPEAN PAINTINGS

Although smaller than its collection of sculptures, The Glyptotek's collection of European paintings is extraordinary in its diversity and quality; featuring works by Picasso, Delacroix, Van Gogh, Toulouse-Lautrec, Vuillard, and Gauguin. Edouard Manet's two works *The Execution of the Emperor Maximilian* (1867) and *The Absinthe Drinker* (1859) are particularly impressive.

## 360 THE (UNUSUAL) MASTERPIECES

The Glyptotek's collection contains, unquestionably, priceless masterpieces. But some of the most interesting pieces are those that are the most unusual. For example: the 3000-year-old wooden hippopotamus carving, the *Nasothek* (broken noses collection), the Hellenistic sculpture of a sleeping negro boy, the bronze of a tiger battling a crocodile, Max Ernst's surrealist painting *Portrait of Gala Eluard*, *L'idole*, and Kai Nelson's beautiful and bizarre *Water Mother* fountain statuary.

## *The 5 best*
# NON-ART MUSEUMS

361 **OPEN AIR MUSEUM (FRILANDSMUSEET)**
**Kongevejen 100**
**Kongens Lyngby** ⑧
**+45 4120 6455 (summer)**
**+45 3313 4411 (winter)**
*www.natmus.dk*

This free outdoor museum gives visitors the opportunity to step back into Denmark's agricultural and domestic past. The museum's more than 50 historic homes, farms, and gardens have been set up to both preserve and celebrate traditional country life. Also make sure to visit the adjacent Brede Works factory and housing.

362 **KAREN BLIXEN MUSEUM**
**Rungsted Strandvej 111**
**Rungsted Kyst** ⑧
**+45 4557 1057**
*www.blixen.dk*

Just north of Copenhagen, in the harbour town of Rungsted, is Rungstedlund, the home of beloved Danish author Karen Blixen (1885-1962). Blixen's home has been preserved and converted into a museum celebrating her life, writings and drawings, and her travels abroad.

### 363 THE DANISH JEWISH MUSEUM

**Proviantpassagen 6**
**Copenhagen K** ①
**+45 3311 2218**
*www.jewmus.dk*

In October of 1943, the Danish Resistance, along with ordinary Danish citizens, coordinated the mass rescue of over 7000 Danish Jews before they could be arrested during the Nazi occupation of Denmark. Designed by renowned architect Daniel Libeskind, The Danish Jewish Museum highlights this, as well as many other stories of the Jewish experience in Denmark.

### 364 OLD CARLSBERG BREWERY

**Gamle Carlsberg Vej 11**
**Copenhagen V** ③
**+45 3327 1282**
*www.visitcarlsberg.dk*

The site of the first Carlsberg Brewery, founded by J.C. Jacobsen 1847, is now home to the Visit Carlsberg experience, where beer lovers can get a first hand look at how beer was brewed in the 19th century, browse the museum's collection of 20.000 glass bottles, and meet the brewery's horses.

### 365 MARITIME MUSEUM OF DENMARK

**Ny Kronborgvej 1**
**Helsingør** ⑧
**+45 4921 0685**
*www.mfs.dk*

From the Vikings to Maersk Shipping, the story of Denmark is the story of a people learning to master life at sea. Opened in 2014, the award-winning Maritime Museum of Denmark is well worth the trip north from Copenhagen, especially when coupled with a visit to nearby Kronborg Castle.

# The 5 best places to see
# LIVE MUSIC

366 **VEGA**
**Enghavevej 40**
**Copenhagen V ③**
**+45 3325 7011**
*www.vega.dk*

VEGA is actually four venues, with capacities ranging from the 1550-person 'Stor VEGA' hall down to the cosy 250-person 'Ideal Bar' venue. Some of the biggest names to perform at VEGA include David Bowie, Prince, Moby, Norah Jones, and Foo Fighters.

367 **PUMPEHUSET**
**Studiestræde 52**
**Copenhagen K ①**
**+45 3393 1960**
*www.pumpehuset.dk*

With two separate halls for hosting live concerts, Pumpehuset (the pump house) is a repurposed, historic water supply facility from the 19th century. It is known as a place to see louder, 'harder', and a more diverse range of shows.

368 **DR KONCERTHUSET**
**Ørestads Boulevard 13**
**Copenhagen S ⑦**
*www.dr.dk/Koncerthuset*

Designed by Pritzker-Prize-winning architect Jean Nouvel and completed in 2009, the DR Koncerthuset is now the home of the Danish National Symphony Orchestra, and also hosts concerts from all genres.

## 369 LOPPEN

Sydområdet 4B
Christianshavn ②
+45 3257 8422
*www.loppen.dk*

Loppen (the flea) is Freetown Christiania's rawest, most energised live music venue. Featuring local, regional, and international acts, Loppen is an intimate, rustic, 'no frills' venue that specialises in alternative, punk, and other high-intensity shows.

## 370 HUSET KBH CULTURE CENTRE

Rådhusstræde 13
Copenhagen K ①
+45 2151 2151
*www.huset-kbh.dk*

Huset KBH is such a cool place – a diverse, friendly venue existing for the sole purpose of putting on art, literature, cinema, and music events in the heart of the city, about 1500 per year. There is always something going on here, and when it comes to live music, Huset hosts all sorts: local and regional artists, tribute bands, jazz, rock, techno and everything in between.

368 DR KONCERTHUSET

# *The 5 best*
# CONTEMPORARY ART
## *galleries*

---

371 **GALLERY POULSEN**
Flæsketorvet 24
Copenhagen V ③
+45 3333 9396
*www.gallerypoulsen.com*

Located in Copenhagen's fashionable Meatpacking District, Gallery Poulsen focuses on showing the work of international artists who create visual narratives on either paper or canvas.

372 **OXHOLM GALLERY**
Ravnsborggade 5-6
Copenhagen N ④
+45 2341 2333
*www.gallerioxholm.dk*

This contemporary gallery is located in the heart of the Nørrebro district, on the vibrant Ravnsborggade. Oxholm contains two distinct showrooms: the 'Room' and the 'Hall', both of which feature the work of established and rising artists. The Gallery is open Tuesday through Sunday afternoons.

373 **SECHER FINE ART & DESIGN**
Bredgade 25
Copenhagen K ①
+45 2427 7038
*www.secherfineart.com*

The Secher gallery's living-room-style interiors feature furniture by Hans Wegner, lamps by Poul Henningsen, and a wide range of modern paintings. Open Tuesday through Saturday afternoons.

### 374 PETER LAV GALLERY

Bredgade 65A
Copenhagen K ①
+45 2880 2398
*www.plgallery.dk*

The mission of the Peter Lav Gallery is to 'promote and further the careers of emerging artists who are exploring the boundaries of the photographic media'. To the end, the Peter Lav Gallery is continually showing impressive and provocative photographic works in this somewhat hidden building. Open Tuesday through Saturday afternoons.

### 375 GALLERI NICOLAI WALLNER

Ny Carlsberg Vej 68
Copenhagen V ③
+45 3257 0970
*www.nicolaiwallner.com*

Housed in an impressive, 800-square-metre repurposed garage space, Galleri Nicolai Wallner is one of the largest contemporary art spaces in Copenhagen. Exhibitions here show works on paper or canvas, photography, paintings, large-scale installations, sculpture, and performance art from local and international artists.

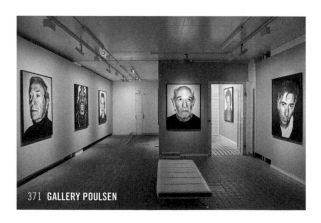

371 GALLERY POULSEN

# The 5 most epic works of
# PUBLIC SCULPTURE

---

### 376 THE ARTEMIS FOUNTAIN
**Hans Tavsens Park**
**Hans Tavsens Gade**
**Copenhagen N** ④

At the heart of Nørrebro's lovely Hans Tavsens Park is this striking Artemis fountain, completed in 1934. Designed by Danish sculptor Johannes Bjerg (1886-1955), the fountain's centrepiece depicts Artemis, the Greek goddess of the hunt.

### 377 GEFION FOUNTAIN
**Churchillparken**
**Copenhagen K** ①

Erected in 1908, the impressive Gefion Fountain is one the largest works of public art in Copenhagen. Based on a 9th-century poem, the fountain depicts the Norse goddess Gefion driving a powerful team of beasts while she works to create Zealand, the Danish island upon which Copenhagen is located.

### 378 A MOMENT OF PERIL
**Kongens Have**
**Øster Voldgade 4**
**Copenhagen K** ①

One of the most dramatic and unusual public sculptures in Copenhagen, *A Moment of Peril* is a copy of an original work by the Englishman Sir Thomas Brock (1847-1922). It depicts an American Indian, on horseback, battling a great serpent with a spear.

380 THE ELEPHANT GATE AND TOWER

### 379 STATUE OF BISHOP ABSALON
**Højbro Plads**
**Copenhagen K** ①

This epic equestrian statue commemorates the man traditionally acknowledged as the founder of Copenhagen. An advisor to King Valdemar I of Denmark, Absalon (1128-1201) helped expand the territories of the Danish kingdom, spread Christianity, and established the first fortified city of Copenhagen aroudn 1167.

### 380 THE ELEPHANT GATE AND TOWER
**Ny Carlsberg Vej 140**
**Copenhagen V** ③

Commissioned by the brewery giant Carl Jacobsen in 1901, The Elephant Gate at the Carlsberg Brewery was designed by architect Vilhelm Dahlerup. It features four life-size elephants, which hold up the tower above them. Look for the initials of Jacobsen's four children (Theodora, Vagn, Helge and Paula) inscribed on the elephants.

# The 5 best places to
# WATCH A FILM

---

### 381 THE GRAND THEATRE
Mikkel Bryggers Gade 8
Copenhagen K ①
+45 3315 1611
*www.grandteatret.dk*

With its richly ornate interiors, classy wine bar and cafe, and a specialized focus on arthouse and world films, this independently-operated cinema offers guests the opportunity to escape from the tourist crowds of summer or the cold winds of winter and take in a film in true style.

### 382 GLORIA BIOGRAF & CAFÉ
Rådhuspladsen 59
Copenhagen V ③
+45 3312 4292
*www.gloria.dk*

Located in the very heart of the city centre is the tiny Gloria cinema. With only one screen, the quaint, quirky Gloria specializes in independent films from around the world and offers visitors a truly intimate movie experience.

### 383 VESTER VOV VOV
Absalonsgade 5
Copenhagen V ③
+45 3324 4200
*www.vestervovvov.dk*

First opened in 1975, Vester Vov Vov was an independent cinema founded by movie lovers, for movie lovers. These days, this art cinema and cafe has stayed true to its roots and is a great place to catch both offbeat arthouse movies or mainstream films that are no longer showing in the larger cinemas.

### 384 EMPIRE BIO

**Guldbergsgade 29**
**Copenhagen N ④**
+45 3536 0036
*www.empirebio.dk*

This low-key neighbourhood cinema is rarely over-crowded and has recently been renovated. A special bonus of movie watching at the Empire Bio: the oversized cinema seats and extra leg room.

### 385 DFI FILMHOUSE

**Danish Film Institute**
**Gothersgade 55**
**Copenhagen K ①**
+45 3374 3412
*www.dfi.dk*

The Danish Film Institute features an extensive film, stills, and poster archive, a bookshop, and – best of all – three cinemas that screen over 60 films a month, many of which are in English or will feature English subtitles.

385 **DFI**

TOWER PLAYGROUND

# 20 THINGS TO DO WITH CHILDREN

## *The 5 most magical*
# URBAN PLAYGROUNDS

386 **THE BERMUDA TRIANGLE IN NØRREBRO PARK**
Stefansgade 28-30
Copenhagen N ④
+45 3585 2271

Designed by Danish playground masters Monstrum, the 'Bermuda Triangle' is the perfect place to let kids' feet and imaginations run wild. The playground features a crashed airplane, a pirate ship, a row-boat, and a surfacing whale. All safe for supervised climbing.

387 **BRUMLEBYEN PLAYGROUND**
Brumlebyen, enter at Østerbrogade 55A
Copenhagen Ø ⑤

Brumlebyen is one of Copenhagen's most interesting preserved historic neighbourhoods. And tucked away deep inside this charming, yellow-walled community is a magically crooked, twisting 'mini-Brumlebyen' kids space that playfully mimics the architecture of the area around it. Features slides, rope bridge, climbing walls, and playhouses, but no public facilities.

### 388 SKYDEBANEN PLAYGROUND

Absalonsgade 12
Copenhagen V ③
+45 3323 1859

Walled-off between the busy streets of Vesterbrogade and Istegade is the beloved but hidden Skydebanen Park. Along with sandy areas, slides, swings and tunnels, the highlight of this playground is the colourful, oversized wooden parrot which stands guard over the park and the historic Museum of Copenhagen behind it.

### 389 HAUSER PLADS PLAYGROUND

Hauser Plads 16
Copenhagen K ①

This quirky, centrally located play space features swings, a sand pit, and all kinds of objects to climb on and jump off. And even though this playground is situated in the very heart of the city centre, its secure design allows kids the freedom to run wild and parents to rest easy during a shopping or sightseeing break.

### 390 NIKOLAJ PLADS PLAYGROUND

Nikolaj Plads 5-11
Copenhagen K ①

Built as a part of Copenhagen's 'Art Playground' programme, the colourful, forest-themed play space at Nikolaj Plads is located right off the Strøget (Copenhagen's busiest shopping street) and offers kids a welcome playcation during their tour of Copenhagen. Tip: see if you can spot the playground's famous wooden owl.

# The 5 best
# ICE CREAM
## shops

───────

### 391 SICILIANSK IS

Skydebanegade 3
Copenhagen V ③
+45 3022 3089
*www.sicilianskis.dk*

Organic ingredients, creative seasonal flavours, and a friendly neighbourhood vibe have made this authentic Sicilian-style gelato shop a Vesterbro favourite. But like most ice cream shops in Copenhagen, Siciliansk Is is only open from April to September.

### 392 ISTID

Jægersborggade 13
Copenhagen N ④
+45 6131 1834
*www.istid.dk*

ISTID is the first and only all organic, nitrogen-chilled ice cream shop in Copenhagen. Part science lab, part performance art space, ISTID was opened by two local women looking to do something new for their fellow ice cream-obsessed Copenhageners.

### 393 OLUFS IS

Olufsvej 6
Copenhagen Ø ⑤
+45 5151 6868
*www.olufs.dk*

OLUFs IS was the first shop in Copenhagen to make specialty, handmade ice lollies. They call them 'ice sticks' here, and with over 30 flavours in rotation, there is always something new and delicious to discover.

### 394 VAFFELBAGEREN AND RAJISSIMO

Nyhavn 49
+45 3314 0698
*www.vaffelbageren.dk*
Nyhavn 19
+45 5052 7629
*www.rajissimo.dk*
Copenhagen K ①

There is no more quintessential Copenhagen experience than wandering the cobblestone streets of Nyhavn with a giant waffle cone stuffed with ice cream in your hand. Lucky for you, there are two excellent options along Nyhavn for freshly made cones and classicly flavoured scoops of ice cream.

### 395 ØSTERBERG ICE CREAM

Rosenvængets Allé 7C
Copenhagen Ø ⑤
+45 6142 3289
*www.osterberg-ice.dk*

Cathrine Østerberg's shop is a rising star among Copenhagen's craft ice cream scene. With her mission to help customers 'taste the world', Cathrine offers all natural ice creams and sorbets in intriguing flavours such as aloe vera with pomegranate and red dragon fruit.

393 OLUFS IS

# The 5 coolest
# SHOPS FOR KIDS

396 **LEGO FLAGSHIP STORE COPENHAGEN**
Vimmelskaftet 37
Copenhagen K ①
+45 5215 9158
www.lego.com

Based out of Billund, Denmark, LEGO is one of the most recognizable brand names in the world, especially among children. The colourful LEGO Flagship Store is part interactive play space, part LEGO paradise.

397 **GYNGEHESTEN**
Margrethevej 1
Hellerup ⑧
+45 3961 0509
www.gyngehesten.dk

Gyngehesten (the rocking horse) may be the most delightful shop in all of Copenhagen. Every inch of the shop is stocked with a magical selection of charming children's toys, games, plush animals, and books, many of which are made in Scandinavia.

398 **MILIBE COPENHAGEN**
Gammel Kongevej 92
Frederiksberg ⑥
+45 3325 1144
www.milibecopenhagen.dk

Founded in 2002 by designers Maria Raben and Mille Milt, Milibe is kids fashion that focuses on the classics: modern prints, simple stripes, and soft, durable fabrics.

### 399 TINDERBOX KIDS
AT WATERFRONT
SHOPPING CENTRE
Philip Heymans Allé 17
Hellerup ⑧
+45 2049 7505
www.tinderbox-kids.dk

The Waterfront Shopping Centre in Hellerup actually boasts two colourful Tinderbox Kids stores, one for fashion and another for games and toys. The kidswear shop carries inspiring collections of clothes from Scandinavian brands such as Bang Bang Copenhagen, Little Remix, Soft Gallery, and Petit Nord.

### 400 BARNLIL' COPENHAGEN
Smallegade 34
Frederiksberg ⑥
+45 3311 9016
www.barnlil.dk

Another great shop for kids in Frederiksberg is Barnlil' Copenhagen. With its range of quirky, cool kids fashion, shoes, toys, and interior design items, Barnlil' could be described as a 'lifestyle shop' for Copenhagen's future hipsters and creative geniuses.

## *The 5 best places for*
# INTERACTIVE
# LEARNING

---

### 401 TRAFFIC PLAYGROUND

Gunner Nu Hansens
Plads 10
Copenhagen Ø ⑤
+45 3542 3708
*www.kk.dk/*
*trafiklegepladsen*

As one of the world's most bicycle-friendly cities, Copenhagen takes cycle safety very seriously. This playground was created as a place to help kids learn the rules of the road and get a chance to practice their bicycle skills in a realistic but car-free area.

### 402 TOWER PLAYGROUND

Frederik V's Vej 4
Copenhagen Ø ⑤
+45 3366 3472

Copenhagen is a great city for play-based learning, and nowhere is better than the Tower Playground, where kids can play, slide, climb, and run amok in the shadow of the city's five most famous towers, all replicated here in miniature.

### 403 KLATRESKOVEN

Pasteursvej 8-10
Copenhagen V ③
+45 2894 4648
*www.klatreskoven.dk*

This urban climbing forest is a great place for kids, and parents, to practice their balance, agility, and exercise a bit of courage. With unique adventure courses for every skill level, one near the ground for little kids and others higher up for older kids.

## 404 THE COPENHAGEN ZOO

Roskildevej 32
Frederiksberg ⑥
+45 7220 0200
*www.zoo.dk*

Featuring a tropical butterfly house, a children's petting zoo, the 'world of primates,' the zoo tower overlooking the city, and the world-famous indoor Elephant House (designed by architect Norman Foster) the Copenhagen Zoo never fails to incite wonder in kids of all ages.

## 405 THE GUARD'S FORT

Garderhøjfort 4
Gentofte ⑧
+45 3965 6179
*www.garderhojfort.dk*

With interactive exhibits designed by the city's popular Experimentarium education group, Garderhøjfortet (the Guard's Fort) is an opportunity for families to step back in time and experience 19th-century Danish military life. Here kids can tour the 360-degree cannon, practise decoding secret messages, and play in the indoor gym.

TATTOO PARLOUR
CINEMA Lounge
SELF-SERVICE KITCHEN
LOCKERS

# 15 PLACES
# TO SLEEP

## *The 5 best*
# BOUTIQUE HOTELS

**406 HOTEL SP34**

Sankt Peders Stræde 34
Copenhagen K ⓘ
+45 3313 3000
www.brochner-hotels.dk/
our-hotels/sp34

Opened in 2014, this boutique hotel has impeccable style: modern interiors, Danish designed furnishings, and an all-around minimalistic, Scandinavian vibe. The bedrooms are small but the common spaces are generous, stylish, and cosy.

**407 HOTEL SKT. PETRI**

Krystalgade 22
Copenhagen K ⓘ
+45 3345 9100
www.sktpetri.com

Named for the nearby Church of Saint Peter, this cool, modernist hotel is well-positioned in Copenhagen's Latin Quarter. A stay here comes with all the amenities you'd expect from a boutique hotel, plus an excellent bar, restaurant, and summer-ready courtyard.

**408 IBSENS HOTEL**

Vendersgade 23
Copenhagen K ⓘ
+45 3345 7744
www.arthurhotels.dk/dk/
ibsens-hotel

Ibsens is a prime location for travelers hoping to explore the Nørrebro, Vesterbro, and Frederiksberg districts, as well as the city centre. Also the Copenhagen lakes and the Torvehallerne food market are very close at hand.

### 409 CENTRAL HOTEL

Tullinsgade 1
Copenhagen V ③
+45 3321 0095
www.centralhotelogcafe.dk

It doesn't get more boutique than the quaint, one-room Central Hotel, located just around the corner from one of Vesterbro's hippest streets. This idiosyncratic little inn is an Instagrammer's dream, but if you really want to stay here, you better book the room way ahead of time.

### 410 HOTEL ALEXANDRA

H.C. Andersens
Boulevard 8
Copenhagen K ①
+45 3374 4444
www.hotelalexandra.dk

A self-described 'lifestyle hotel', the Alexandra was fully renovated in 2013 and has a very distinct, high-end retro aesthetic. With private and common rooms ornamented with Danish designed chairs, art, and textiles from the 1950s, 1960s, and 1970s, the Alexandra Hotel is classically vintage in all the right ways.

406 HOTEL SP34

# *The 5*

# HIPPEST HOSTELS

---

### 411 URBAN HOUSE

Colbjørnsensgade 5-11
Copenhagen V ③
+45 3323 2929
www.urbanhouse.me

Urban House has a lot to offer guests: bike rentals, a tattoo parlour, an in house cinema, a live music stage, and a busy bar. The bedrooms here are simple but clean, which is fine because staying at this place is all about the fun community atmosphere anyway.

### 412 SLEEP IN HEAVEN

Struenseegade 7
Copenhagen N ④
+45 3535 4648
www.sleepinheaven.com

This vibrant backpacker hostel is located in the shabby-chic Nørrebro district. The services and amenities here are pretty standard for an European hostel, but the atmosphere is lively and the neighbourhood feels authentic.

### 413 GENERATOR HOSTEL

Adelgade 5
Copenhagen K ①
+45 7877 5400
www.generatorhostels.com/
copenhagen

The highly-rated Generator Hostel is a hip, funky hostel that feels more like a concept hotel than a traditional backpackers haunt (ie: no guest kitchens). Note: Adelsgade is a great access point for Copenhagen's city centre, located just a few steps away from The King's Garden, the colourful Nyhavn harbour, some of the city's best bistros, and the main shopping areas.

414 **COPENHAGEN DOWNTOWN HOSTEL**

Vandkunsten 5
Copenhagen K ①
+45 7023 2110
www.copenhagen
downtown.com

Currently rated as Copenhagen's best hostel (via HostelWorld.com), CDH also boasts the city's best address for hostel dwellers, right in the centre of the city. On top of the stellar location, CDH offers loads of amenities: free family-style dinners every night, free walking tours, happy hours, cheap 'all you can eat breakfast', and live music events.

415 **WOODAH HOSTEL**

Abel Cathrines Gade 1
Copenhagen V ③
+45 2390 5563
www.woodah-hostel.com

This small 'yoga hostel' offers guests a tranquil option to the typical bustling hostel scene. With its relaxed vibe, Woodah is well-suited for the bohemian Vesterbro district.

411 **URBAN HOUSE**

# *The 5 most*
# LUXURIOUS HOTELS

---

416 **RADISSON BLU ROYAL**
Hammerichsgade 1
Copenhagen K ①
+45 3342 6000
www.radissonblu.com/en/
royalhotel-copenhagen

This hotel, designed by architect Arne Jacobsen in the late 1950s, is an icon of Danish modernism. And though the hotel has been fully updated for the 21st century, the spirit of mid-century modernism still lives in room 606, which retains the original 1960s Jacobsen decor.

417 **SKOVSHOVED HOTEL**
Strandvejen 267
Charlottenlund ⑧
+45 3964 0028
www.skovshovedhotel.com

Skovshoved Hotel is an elegant example of an old-fashioned, seaside 'bathing hotel'. It is located halfway between two of the best beaches on the 'Danish Riviera': Charlottenlund Fort Beach and Bellevue Beach.

418 **AVENUE HOTEL**
Åboulevard 29
Frederiksberg ④
+45 3537 3111
www.avenuehotel.dk

The stylish, 68-room Avenue Hotel was fully renovated in 2005 and is positioned at the border between the equally noteworthy Nørrebro and Frederiksberg districts. With its 19th-century red brick architecture and posh interiors, the Avenue Hotel is one of the most fashionable accommodations in Copenhagen.

### 419 COPENHAGEN ADMIRAL HOTEL

Toldbodgade 24-28
Copenhagen K ①
+45 3374 1414
www.admiralhotel.dk

Located directly on the water, just around the corner from the Royal Palace of Amalienborg, the Copenhagen Admiral Hotel is steeped in over 200 years of rich, local history. With over 300 unique rooms, this award-winning, four-star hotel is also rich in stylish, beam-trimmed Scandinavian ambiance.

### 420 HOTEL D'ANGLETERRE

Kongens Nytorv 34
Copenagen K ①
+45 3312 0095
www.dangleterre.com

Since 1755, this grand hotel has played hosts to royals, dignitaries, and celebrities. Today, Hotel d'Angleterre stands as a – recently renovated – monument to the golden age of travel and luxury. With its gorgeous rooms and suites, exceptional services, and prime location on the city's most famous square, there is no more luxurious place to stay in Copenhagen.

CHRISTIANSHAVN CANAL

# 40 ACTIVITIES
# FOR WEEKENDS

---

# *The 5 most beautiful*
# WALKS IN THE WOODS

---

### 421 JÆGERSBORG DYREHAVE

Dyrehaven
Klampenborg ⑧
+45 3997 3900

This wild woodland was once the royal hunting grounds of the Danish nobility. Today, the Dyrehaven is by far the largest public park in the Copenhagen area (covering over 11 square kilometres) and is, as its name suggests, full of wildlife: red foxes, hundreds of free-roaming deer, and lots of riders on horseback.

### 422 CHARLOTTENLUND PALACE PARK

Charlottenlund ⑧

Located along the coastal road, the forest park surrounding the stunning Charlottenlund Palace is a hidden woodland gem just north of Copenhagen. With the sea to the east and the charming village of Charlottenlund to the west, this forest of winding paths, giant trees and quiet serenity is just waiting to be explored.

### 423 BERNSTORFF PALACE WOODS

Jægersborg Allé 93
Gentofte ⑧
+45 3963 1080
*www.bernstorffslot.dk*

Bernstorff Palace woods has something for everyone: a traditional tearoom (open only in summer), a horse training facility, a duck pond, rose gardens, and even a working orchard.

### 424 SORGENFRI PALACE PARK

Kongevejen 2
Lyngby ⑧
+45 3395 4200

Tucked away in the village of Lyngby is the dramatic Sorgenfri Palace woods, a rambling, hilly, public forest along the backside of the 18th-century Sorgenfri (free of sorrows) Palace. A walk along the babbling creeks of these idyllic woods is the perfect natural contrast to the lively shopping atmosphere of nearby Lyngby.

### 425 KALVEBOD COMMONS

Granatvej 1-15
Kastrup ⑧
+45 7254 3000

This wilderness area was completely under water until 1938, when it was drained and reclaimed for military use. In 2010, this expansive wetland was opened to the public as a nature preserve and now offers access to breathtaking views, unique animal habitats, cycle paths and artist Alfio Bonanno's iconic *Amager Ark* art installation.

423 BERNSTORFF PALACE WOODS

# The 5 most interesting
# SUBURBS
## to explore

---

**426 HILLERØD**

A short train ride north of Copenhagen is the charming medieval town of Hillerød, home to Frederiksborg Castle, the largest Renaissance palace in Scandinavia. The castle is built on an island surrounded by a moat, scenic lake, and Denmark's most famous baroque gardens.

**427 LYNGBY**

A short train ride from the city center, Lyngby has it all: great shopping, designer showrooms, diverse dining options, and the beautiful Sorgenfri Palace and its surrounding woodlands. Not to be missed in Lyngby is the Frilandsmuseet (the Open Air Museum) and a cluster of Danish design showrooms along the main road.

**428 FREDERIKSBERG**

A district bustling with university students and young families, the heart of Frederiksberg is certainly its popular palace, palace gardens, and the adjacent Copenhagen zoo. Not to be missed is the ultra cool shopping street of Værnedamsvej.

### 429 **HELLERUP**

Known as the 'Beverly Hills' of Copenhagen, the suburb of Hellerup has a distinctly international feel. As home to several embassies, consulate offices, and international schools, Hellerup is also the gateway to the northern coast of Zealand. Not to be missed is the charming Hellerup Sailing Club, the modernist architecture of Tuborg Harbour, and the small Oregård Park.

### 430 **NORDHAVN**

This little district is currently undergoing a massive, multi-decade revitalization and has been master-planned to feature some of Copenhagen's most exciting new architecture, attractions, and services. A short bike ride from the iconic Little Mermaid, Nordhavn is an interesting study in the mix of industrial and natural urban design and to get a glimpse of Copenhagen's future.

430 **NORDHAVN**

## *The 5 best ways to*
# GET OUT
# ON THE WATER

---

**431 GOBOAT**

Islands Brygge 10
Copenhagen S ②
+45 4026 1025
*www.goboat.dk*

The Danish-designed Goboats are solar-powered, require no previous experience to operate, make no noise, and are made, in part, from recycled materials. Able to seat up to eight people, these fun little picnic dinghies are a great way to experience the capital's waterways with freedom.

**432 COPENHAGEN CANAL TOUR BY NETTO BOATS**

departs from Holmens Church or Nyhavn
Copenhagen K ①
*www.havnerundfart.dk*

In just an hour, a Copenhagen canal and harbour tour will give you the opportunity to see the city from an otherwise impossible perspective. And the Netto Baadene (Netto Boat) company offers the exact same tour and boats as their competitor at a much better rate.

### 433 KAYAK REPUBLIC

Børskaj 12
Copenhagen K ①
+45 2288 4989
www.kayakrepublic.dk

Depending on your skill level, you may want to contact Kayak Republic ahead of time to confirm whether or not you'll be able to rent and tour the city waterways without a guide. Also, don't miss the Kayak Bar, one of the best places in the city centre for good weather meetups.

### 434 KAYAK POLO BY BRYGGENS KAYAKPOLO

Islands Brygge 18
Copenhagen S ②
+45 2533 1666
www.bryggens-kajakpolo.dk

Kayak Polo is exactly what it sounds like: teams of individuals in kayaks, trying to simultaneously catch, row and throw. A mixture of handball and bumper boats, this harbour sport is almost as much fun to watch as it is to play.

### 435 SWAN BOATS AT KAFFESALONE

Peblinge Dossering 6
Copenhagen N ④
+45 3535 1219,
www.kaffesalonen.com

Kaffesalonen is a cosy, lakeside cafe in Nørrebro, just across Dronning Louises Bridge from the city centre. Along with a hearty meal on the cafe's sunny terrace or dock-seating area, Kaffesalonen also offers boat rentals: choose between a traditional pedal boat, a rowboat, or, for a more memorable day on the lake, hire a giant, pedal-powered swan boat.

*The 5 best places to*

# GET FIT

---

### 436 KILDESKOVSHALLEN

Adolphsvej 25
Gentofte ⑧
+45 3977 4400
*www.kildeskovshallen.
gentofte.dk*

This large, modern community centre is tucked away in a woodland area north of Copenhagen and very near Bernstorffsvej station. Featuring handball courts, an excellent cafe, lovely gardens, a 25-metre pool, a 50-metre pool, saunas, and a baby swimming basin, Kildeskovshallen is the perfect place to spend a rainy Danish day.

### 437 FREDERIKSBERG SWIMMING HALL

Helgesvej 29
Frederiksberg ⑥
+45 3814 0400
*www.svoemmehal.
frederiksberg.dk*

Like Kildeskovshallen, the cornerstone of Frederiksberg swimming hall is its excellent pool facilities and slide. But, in addition to the pools, this historic centre also has an excellent, reasonably-priced health spa, which features hot tubs, a salt water bath, saunas, massage chairs, and cold water pools. Tip: to ensure you get in, book spa space ahead of time.

## 438 PRISMEN

Holmbladsgade 71
Copenhagen S ⑦
+45 8233 4520
*www.prismen.kk.dk*

Completed in 2006, the striking, all-glass architecture of Prismen sets it apart from the gray brick of the surrounding neighbourhood. Inside the Prismen (the prism) is a large, multi-use arena for basketball, football, dance classes, martial arts, and free play for kids. Tip: call ahead to see when the arena has 'open hall', as the arena is sometimes booked for special events.

## 439 GAME STREETMEKKA

Enghavevej 82D
Valby ⑥
+45 3323 6665

Streetmekka is the best indoor gym in Copenhagen for 'pickup' basketball. Created as a social youth initiative to foster positive relationships within the community, there are friendly games happening here at all hours. To get access, stop at the reception and 'join' the gym – for a small fee – and then introduce yourself and start ballin' it up with the locals.

## 440 FÆLLEDPARKEN

Edel Sauntes Allé
Copenhagen Ø ⑤
+45 3366 3366

First opened back in 1914, Fælledparken is located in Østerbro, just beside Parken (Denmark's national sports stadium), and is Copenhagen's largest public park. What makes Fælledparken so good for fitness is the park's generous number of running/walking trails, basketball courts, football pitches, playgrounds, and skate park. Beginners and experts welcome.

# *The 5 best places to*
# DANCE
# THE NIGHT AWAY

---

### 441 BAKKEN KBH
Flæsketorvet 19
Copenhagen V ③
*www.bakkenkbh.dk*

Bakken is the Meatpacking District's most consistently crowded club. Powered by cheap beer, talented DJs, and an all-around friendly vibe, Bakken is a graffiti-tagged, unpretentious dive club where locals of every flavour gather to get down. Check the club's event page to see what's happening.

### 442 ZEFSIDE
Frederiksholms Kanal 4
Copenhagen K ①
+45 2846 8987
*www.zefside.dk*

Thursday, Friday, and Saturday nights, this basement cocktail bar is one contiguous party, attracting the after party crowd (Zefside stays open until 4 am). Though the dancefloor here takes a somewhat ambiguous form, there's no resisting the contagious beats of Zefside's DJs, who specialize in helping transform the whole place into a dance party. Tip: lots of happy hour specials.

## 443 RUST

Guldbergsgade 8
Copenhagen N ④
+45 3524 5200
www.rust.dk

Located on a shabby-chic side street in Nørrebro, Rust functions as both a concert venue and a multi-floor dance club. Rust offers a mix of music on its three floors and regularly features visits by well known local and celebrity DJs.

## 444 CULTURE BOX

Kronprinsessegade 54
Copenhagen K ①
+45 3332 5050
www.culture-box.com

This electronica club has four distinct 'boxes' in which to experience the throb and energy of DJ-driven beats. Founded in 2005, Culture Box is a two-floor club that draws impressive queues almost every weekend, especially for highly-anticipated special events.

## 445 JOLENE BAR

Flæsketorvet 81-85
Copenhagen V ③

Another dive-style club located in the Meatpacking District, Jolene is more diverse and more relaxed than the typical techno-pounding Euro night spot. Decked out in the shabby chic style that has come to epitomize the Copenhagen scene, Jolene is sometimes an electronica club, sometimes a rock club, sometimes something else entirely, but always guaranteed to be a good time.

## The 5 most charming

# WALKS ALONG THE WATER

---

**446 CHRISTIANSHAVN CANAL**
Christianshavn ②

Inspired by the cities of Holland, the Danish King Christian IX built the canals of Christianshavn in the 17th century. Today, wandering along Christianshavn Canal is one of the best ways to experience Copenhagen's nautical history and modern local flavour.

**447 COPENHAGEN LAKES**
Østerbro, Nørrebro,
Vesterbro Districts
Copenhagen K ①

Copenhagen's five man-made lakes stretch like a watery belt across three of the city's central districts: from cosy Østerbro in the north, through the artsy district of Nørrebro, and into the vibrant neighbourhood of Vesterbro to the south.

**448 ISLANDS BRYGGE HARBOUR WALK**
Southern District
Christianshavn ②

Crossing over the harbour from the city centre on Langebro Bridge, turn south into Islands Brygge. Moving south through Islands Brygge (Iceland's Quay), walkers will have excellent views back toward the city before arriving at the impressive Gemini Residence building.

## 449 THE STRANDVEJEN

**Suburban District**
**Strandvejen** ⑧

On sunny days, the oversized waterfront sidewalk stretching between Charlottenlund Beach Park and Bellevue Beach will be packed with Copenhageners. With views of busy sailboats, the historic Skovshoved fishing village, and Sweden on the horizon, you can see why locals are eager to trek these four scenic kilometres, then turn around and do it again.

## 450 NYHAVN TO THE LITTLE MERMAID

**City Centre**
**Copenhagen K** ①

Turning north from Nyhavn onto Toldbodgade/Amaliegade will start walkers on a two kilometre seafront journey that passes by some of the city's most iconic landmarks, including Amalienborg (the Queen's home), the Marble Church, the New Royal Opera House, St. Alban's Church, and ending up at *The Little Mermaid* statue.

## *The 5 best*
# SUMMER FESTIVALS
## *to attend*

---

### 451 COPENHAGEN DISTORTION
first week of June

Unlike any other summer event in the city, the electronica-fueled Copenhagen Distortion is a massive mobile festival that includes street events throughout the Nørrebro and Vesterbro districts and culminates with a final party in Copenhagen Harbour. Distortion is a self-described celebration of 'international club culture' expressed through, 'a week of emerging dance music and orchestrated chaos'.

### 452 COPENHAGEN JAZZ FESTIVAL
first week of July

Since the 1950s and 1960s, Copenhagen has been a destination for some of the world's best jazz players. And ever since the 1970s, for ten days in July, artists from both the traditional and experimental schools – and everything in between – occupy the city's bars, cafes, streets, and parks, filling the capital with an eclectic array of jazz stylings. Tip: many of the cafe and outdoor performances are free.

### 453 ZULU SOMMERBIO
free outdoor movies in the park, early August

Every August, Danish broadcaster TV 2 Zulu sponsors a series of free, open-air film screenings shown in the city's public parks. Each of the Zulu Sommerbio films are recent cinema releases and are shown in their original language with Danish subtitles. Tip: bring a blanket, a bottle of wine, and enjoy a movie under the stars.

### 454 SHAKESPEARE AT HAMLET'S CASTLE
early August
*www.hamletscenen.dk*

Ever since 1816, when a group of Danish soldiers initiated the tradition of performing Hamlet inside of Kronborg Castle, summer in Helsingor has been Shakespeare season. Each summer, Kronborg (the castle known as 'Elsinore' in Shakespeare's *Hamlet*) hosts a series of diverse events celebrating the English language's greatest playwright, including open-air dramatic performances, film screenings, and experimental art installations.

### 455 ROSKILDE FESTIVAL
late June or early July,
*www.roskilde-festival.dk*

Created in 1971 as a Woodstock-esque, outdoor music and arts event for that era's hippies, the Roskilde Festival of the 21st century has evolved into the largest music festival in Northern Europe. The annual event, held 40 kilometres southwest of Copenhagen, features international artists and music from across all genres. Roskilde alumni include Bob Marley, Beastie Boys, Bob Dylan, Radiohead, Jay-Z, and Pharrell Williams.

# 5 reasons to visit
# JÆGERSBORG DYREHAVE

Dyrehaven
Klampenborg ⑧
+45 3997 3900

### 456 A UNESCO WORLD HERITAGE WILDERNESS

This massive UNESCO World Heritage site was once the royal hunting grounds of the Danish nobility, but today is Copenhagen's largest and wildest green space. Along with its rolling hills, lakes, streams, and historic buildings, Dyrehave (deer park) is home to over 3000 free-roaming deer and many other species of wildlife.

### 457 PETER LIEPS HUS

Having been destroyed and then rebuilt on numerous occasions, this iconic house has been a part of The Deer Park since the late 1700s. Today, Peter Lieps Hus is the best of the Dyrehaven's cafes, restaurants, and pubs. Located at the central crossroads of the park, just opposite Bakken, Peter Lieps Hus is the ideal stop for an ice cream or a beer during a visit to Dyrehave.

458 **CYCLING IN THE WILD**

The Deer Park is the best place in Copenhagen for a bike ride in nature, as many forest areas in the city do not allow cycling.

459 **BAKKEN**

As the world's oldest (since 1583!), continually-operating amusement park, Bakken has changed considerably over time and, yet, the park still retains a rich, nostalgic atmosphere that keeps locals coming back summer after summer.

460 **THE HISTORIC HUBERTUS HUNT**

Every year since 1900, on the first Sunday of November, Dyrehaven has hosted 'The Hubertus Hunt'. The Hunt is a not an actual fox hunt, but, instead, a cross-country horse race through the park, during which 160 riders and their horses must race 13 kilometres and navigate more than 30 obstacles.

5°C

13:42

HEJ CYKLIST!

Du er nummer

906

I DAG

og nummer

436231

I ÅR

der cykler forbi her

GOD TUR

og tak fordi du cykler i byen!

I ♥ CPH

On this cycle track the City of Copenhagen counts
the number of cyclists who have passed by today (i dag)
and since the beginning of the year (i år)

BIKING IN COPENHAGEN

# 40 INSIGHTS INTO COPENHAGEN

# 5 secrets to life in the
# WORLD'S MOST
# LIVEABLE CITY

### 461 A HAPPY CITY

In 2014, Copenhagen became the first city in the world to be designated by *Monocle Magazine* as 'the world's most liveable city' three times (also in 2008 and 2013). Monocle's quality of life index takes into consideration a city's crime, health care services, economy, education, access to public transport, green spaces, commitment to culture, and hours of sunshine per year.

### 462 AN ACTIVE CITY

In the 1960s, the city government of Copenhagen made a conscious decision to limit the impact that cars would have on the city. Instead, the city planners decided to create more pedestrian-only zones, to build an extensive network of bicycle paths, and to invest in high quality bus and train services.

**463 A BALANCED CITY**

Copenhageners, like all Danes, value a healthy work-life balance. According to the OECD, less than 2% of Danes work 50 hours per week or more (compared to 11% in the USA and 22% in Japan). The national standard is 37 hours of work per week.

**464 AN INNOVATIVE CITY**

The cost of living and various forms of tax in Denmark are high, no question about that. But, on the other hand, the Danish state's social safety nets are generous and plentiful. These safety nets are part of the reason that Copenhageners are so willing to take risks and innovate.

**465 A TRUSTWORTHY CITY**

Low crime rates, low levels of gender inequality, low levels of political corruption – these are all statistical realities of life in Copenhagen. Add to this a general trust in the government, the education system, and the neighbour next door, all of which help to make Danish society a society of trust, where it's even safe to leave your baby in a pram outside of a busy cafe.

# 5

# CULTURAL QUIRKS
## *to know about Denmark and the Danes*

---

**466 FOLLOW THE RULES**

In general, Danes follow the rules, whether by paying their taxes, separating their garbage, or waiting for the cross walk's red lights to turn green. So, if you see a sign in Copenhagen that says 'no bike parking' or 'no smoking' it's a good idea to pay attention and follow the lead of the locals.

**467 A COCONUT CULTURE**

Danes are, in fact, a society of loving, loyal, and compassionate people. Like the sweet, insulated fruit of a coconut, it may take some time to access the heart of Danish culture. But, ultimately, your patience will reap relational rewards.

**468 THE SOUND OF SILENCE**

Day or night, summer and winter, on bustling shopping streets and on public transport alike, you can almost always find some peace and quiet. Unlike many cities, Copenhagen is a place where residents truly value the sound of silence.

## 469 **BABIES LEFT OUTSIDE**

One thing you might see at some point during your time in Copenhagen is a baby (or babies) sleeping in a pram, left alone outside of a cafe or a shop while the parents are dining or shopping inside. This is actually a very common practice and is both a practical necessity (fitting big prams into the city's many small spaces is never easy) and a reflection of what a safe city Copenhagen is.

## 470 **WINTER BATHING**

Everyone knows that Denmark has a cold climate: lots of wind and rain and winter temperatures that often stay below zero for months. But despite this, many Danes are committed to the practice of *vinterbadning* (winter bathing). The locals say this popular ancient ritual keeps the heart pumping, the skin glowing, and the mind refreshed.

470 WINTER BATHING, CHARLOTTENLUND SØBAD

## 5 good-to-know
# DANISH
# WORDS AND PHRASES

**471 HEJ & HEJ HEJ**

Saying '*hej*' is the most common way to say hello in Copenhagen. Luckily, the pronunciation of the Danish greeting is exactly the same as the pronunciation of 'hi' in English. And, even better, '*hej*' is also how you say goodbye in Danish (you can also say '*hej hej*' for goodbye).

**472 TAK, NEJ TAK, MANGE TAK**

The Danes don't have a word for 'please,' so it's important to know how to say thank you. To say thanks, just say '*tak*' (pronounced like the English word 'talk', rhymes with 'chalk'). To say 'no thank you' just add the word '*nej*' (rhymes with 'rye') before '*tak*,' and you get '*nej tak*'. To express 'many thanks', you can say '*mange tak*', (pronounced 'mang-a talk').

## 473 JEG KAN IKKE TALE DANSK

Since pretty much everyone in Denmark speaks English, chances are you won't have to learn many Danish phrases, but if you want to try and impress the locals, you can respond to their Danish greetings or questions by saying, 'I don't speak Danish' (pronounced 'y-aye can ikka tailor dance-k'), which will be their cue to switch over to English. This one is a challenge, but give it a try and you're certain to make a local smile.

## 474 DET ER MEGET HYGGELIGT

The concept of '*hygge*' (pronounced 'hoo-gah'), or cosiness, is very important during the cold, dark, Danish winters. But, luckily, you can find *hygge* in Copenhagen year-round, and when you experience a cosy cafe, an afternoon in the park, or day at the beach with friends, the right phrase to express your feelings is, '*Det er meget hyggeligt*' ('this is so cosy'), pronounced 'day er mal hoo gleet'.

## 475 HAV EN GOD DAG

'Have a good day, have a good evening, or have a good night' are all very cordial ways to say farewell to your new Danish friends. The key part of all three phrases is the first two thirds, '*hav en god...*' (pronounced 'ha ang go...'). Then you just add on which time of day you'd like to specify: '*dag*' for day (pronounced like the English word 'day'), evening is '*aften*' (pronounced 'aft-in'), and night is '*nat*' (rhymes with 'mat').

# The 5 most important
# RULES FOR BIKING
## in Copenhagen

---

**476 USING COPENHAGEN'S BIKE LANES**

In 2015, Copenhagen officially became the most bicycle-friendly city in the world. The two most important rules for using the city's extensive network of bike lanes are (1) always stay to the right unless you are passing someone, and (2) don't do anything so suddenly that it would disrupt the flow of other cyclists and/or cause a crash.

**477 USE THOSE HAND SIGNALS**

To turn right, extend your right arm outward before turning, to let cyclists behind you know what you're about to do. If you're going to turn left, do the same thing and remember to look back over your left shoulder first so you don't cut someone off. If you plan to stop, then raise your left hand up for a few seconds before you stop to alert those cyclists behind you.

## 478 WHAT THE BELL?

All bikes in Copenhagen are required to have a small bell attached to the handle bars. This is the polite Danish way of alerting cyclists ahead that you'd like to pass them. Just lightly ring your bell, the cyclists ahead will move over to the right and allow you to pass. Once you've made your move, then move over to the right yourself and carry on enjoying the freedom of the biking life.

## 479 PARKING AND LOCKING

When you borrow, rent, or buy a bicycle in Copenhagen, make sure you learn how to lock it securely – and always lock your bike in the city, even if you're popping into a shop for two minutes. Also, look out for 'no bike parking' signs in front of some shops and make sure to pay attention when you leave your bike in a massive bike parking area, many bikes look alike.

## 480 LIGHTS ON

It's the law in Copenhagen that all bikes have a functioning white front light and a red back light. It is not uncommon to be stopped by the police and to have your bike checked for the proper safety lights. When cycling at night or in low light, always turn your lights on. If you need to buy bike lights, they are inexpensive and are available in almost all grocery stores, discount shops, and kiosks.

## *The 5 most*
# IMPORTANT DATES
## *in Copenhagen's history*

481 **1443**

In 1443, the kingdom's capital was moved from Roskilde to Copenhagen, less than three centuries after Copenhagen was established by Bishop Absalon. Six years after becoming the new capital of Denmark, Copenhagen's cathedral was the site of the coronation of Christian I in 1449.

482 **1596**

The longest reign of any Danish monarch belonged to that of Christian IV, who became king in 1596 and ruled for 59 productive years. During this time he built many of Copenhagen's most iconic buildings (including Rosenborg Castle and The Round Tower), waged wars, established several new cities throughout Scandinavia, drank excessively, and fathered dozens of children.

483 **1700s**

The 18th century in Copenhagen was a very difficult time, beginning with an outbreak of the Plague in 1711 that wiped out roughly one third of the city's population. In 1728, the northern third of the city was destroyed in a massive four day-long fire. Then, in early 1801, Britain's Admiral Nelson led an attack on the Danish Royal Navy in Copenhagen harbour initiating 'The Battle of Copenhagen'.

484 **1840s**

By 1840, the districts of Vesterbro, Nørrebro and Østerbro had been incorporated into Copenhagen. Then, in 1847, Copenhagen's central train station was built, linking the city to the rest of Europe via rail. That same year J.C. Jacobsen opened Carlsberg Brewery. And, most significantly, on the 5th of June 1849, King Frederik VII signed the *Grundlov*, the first Danish constitution, thus establishing a constitutional monarchy.

485 **1940-1945**

On April 9, 1940 Nazi forces invaded and occupied Denmark, establishing their headquarters in Copenhagen. For five uneasy years, Copenhageners lived under German occupation rule but were able to establish a successful underground Resistance, and, in October of 1943, helped to coordinate the mass rescue of more than 7000 Danish Jews.

## 5 *surprising*
# COPENHAGEN FACTS

---

**486 THE SEAT OF EUROPE'S OLDEST MONARCHY**

Margrethe II, the current queen of Denmark, resides at the palace of Amalienborg in Copenhagen. But the original, unified kingdom of Denmark was founded by the Viking King 'Gorm The Old', during the 10th century. What began as an elected monarchy evolved, during the 1600's, into an hereditary system and then, in 1849, evolved once more into a constitutional monarchy.

**487 THE CAPITAL OF A GLOBAL EMPIRE**

The Danish colonial empire (existing from around the years 1540 to 1940) was once a vast world power controlling approximately 1,2 million square miles of lands in Europe, South America, Africa, and Asia. During this time, Denmark and Norway were a combined nation known as *Statsfædrelandet* (the State's Fatherland) and Copenhagen was the capital of their impressive empire.

## 488 THE BIRTHPLACE OF SEX REASSIGNMENT SURGERY

In September of 1951, Danish doctors at Gentofte hospital performed the first successful sex reassignment surgery on American George Jorgensen, whose parents were Danish. After the successful surgery, Jorgensen returned to America as Christine Jorgensen and spent the rest of her life as an entertainer and transgender rights activist.

## 489 THE FIRST FOR LEGALISED PORNOGRAPHY

In 1967 the Danish government decriminalised the sale of pornographic writings. Two years later, the Danish Parliament in Copenhagen passed the legislation necessary for Denmark to become the first state in modern history to abolish every legal sanction against pornography for adults.

## 490 THE HOME OF THE BICYCLE SUPERHIGHWAY

Since 2012, the city of Copenhagen and the surrounding municipalities have undertaken the ambitious goal of connecting the region with 500 kilometres of interconnected 'bicycle superhighways'. The goal of the superhighway network is to improve cycling infrastructure and to further incentivise Copenhageners to choose cycling as their preferred means of commuting.

*The 5 most*

# BELOVED AUTHORS

*with Copenhagen ties*

---

491 **PETER HØEG**
(1957-PRESENT)

An enigmatic and sometimes controversial author, Copenhagener Peter Høeg's style is hard to categorize. Best known for the multi-generational and magically-realistic *The History of Danish Dreams* (1988) and the crime thriller *Smilla's Sense of Snow* (1992), Høeg's work has been described as both postmodern fiction as well as social criticism.

492 **KAREN BLIXEN**
(1885-1962)

A native of Rungsted, Denmark – just 24 kilometres north of Copenhagen – the author Karen Blixen is best known for her memoir *Out of Africa* (1937) which chronicles her years spent living on a coffee plantation in Kenya. But Blixen was a prolific writer who worked in several genres and whose books *Seven Gothic Tales* (1937), *Winter's Tales* (1942), and *Babette's Feast* (1950) are all considered essential reading.

### 493 MARTIN ANDERSEN NEXØ
(1869-1954)

Journalist, travel writer, and champion of the working class, the socialist writer Martin Andersen Nexø is best known for his four-part *Pelle The Conqueror* stories, published from 1906 till 1910, which depicts the struggles of a father and son as they emigrate from Sweden to Denmark in the 1850s in search of a better life.

### 494 SØREN KIERKEGAARD
(1813-1855)

Known as the first existential philosopher, Søren Kierkegaard was a writer, poet, critic, theologian, and political activist who spent his life and career challenging the status quo and writing dense, powerful prose. If you want to give Kierkegaard a try, start with *Fear and Trembling* (1843).

### 495 HANS CHRISTIAN ANDERSEN
(1805-1875)

Beloved around the world for his fairy tales, such as *The Ugly Duckling* and *The Snow Queen*, H.C. Andersen is the best-known Danish writer of all time. A friend of Dickens, a prolific traveller, and an all-around fascinating individual, Andersen is widely celebrated in Copenhagen as a national hero.

# *The 5 most helpful*
# DIGITAL RESOURCES

---

### 496 REJSEPLANEN TRANSPORT APP
(FREE)
*www.rejseplanen.dk*

*Rejseplanen* is the best resource for planning journeys in Denmark via public transport, including transport by bus, train, and metro lines. Whether you're taking a day trip to the Lousiana Museum in Humlebæk or traveling to and from The Roskilde Festival, you need *Rejseplanen*.

### 497 YR WEATHER APP
(FREE)
*www.yr.no*

Full disclosure: YR is not Danish, it's the official app of the Norwegian Meteorological Institute, but, frankly, yr.no is much more user-friendly than its Danish counterpart, DMI Weather (Danish Meteorological Institute). Plus, along with cleaner, more modern visuals, YR offers users much more info in English. But remember, as the Danes say: "There's no such thing as bad weather, only poor preparation."

**498  SCANDINAVIA STANDARD.COM**

The thoughtful team behind the Scandinavia Standard blog clearly have their finger on the pulse of all things Scandinavian, from design, to fashion, culture, events, and travel. Best of all, the 'Scandi Six' are committed to sharing their passion and considerable insights with Copenhagen's English-speaking residents and visitors.

**499  COPENHAGENIZE.COM**

Copenhagenize.com is the official blog of Copenhagenize Design Company, an urban design consultancy that utilizes, 'design, anthropology, sociology and common sense' to help cities around the world become more bicycle-friendly. If you're interested in the how and why of Copenhagen's urban design successes, you will find much to appreciate at copenhagenize.com.

**500  MURMUR.DK**

It's not always easy for foreigners to penetrate the intricacies and subtleties of Danish culture, politics or society. Fortunately, there's *The Murmur*, Copenhagen's premier long-form English language newspaper and online news source. *The Murmur*'s nuanced and in-depth reporting touches on a wide range of issues, but makes Danish current affairs accessible to a broad, international audience.

# INDEX

# COLOPHON

**The 500 Hidden Secrets of Copenhagen**
Austin Sailsbury – www.austinsails.com

**GRAPHIC DESIGN** — Joke Gossé and Tinne Luyten
**PHOTOGRAPHY** — Tino van den Berg – www.autoexilio.com
**COVER IMAGE** — Cykelslangen © DISSING+WEITLING architecture
**PHOTO'S** — p. 57,101: Tinne Luyten - p. 219: Austin Sailsbury - p. 157,159: Roel Hendrickx

The addresses in this book have been selected after thorough independent
research by the author, in collaboration with Luster Publishers. The selection is
solely based on personal evaluation of the business by the author. Nothing in this
book was published in exchange for payment or benefits of any kind.

D/2016/12.005/4
ISBN 978 94 6058 1762
NUR 506

© 2016, Luster, Antwerp
First reprint, September 2016
www.lusterweb.com
info@lusterweb.com

Printed in Italy by Printer Trento.